THIS IMMORAL TRADE
Slavery in the 21st Century

BARONESS CAROLINE COX
AND
DR JOHN MARKS

MONARCH
BOOKS

Oxford, UK & Grand Rapids, Michigan, USA

First published in the UK in 2006 by Monarch Books
(a publishing imprint of Lion Hudson plc),
Mayfield House, 256 Banbury Road, Oxford OX2 7DH.
Tel: +44 (0)1865 302750   Fax: +44 (0)1865 302757
Email: monarch@lionhudson.com
www.lionhudson.com

ISBN-13: 978-1-85424-765-0 (UK)
ISBN-10: 1-85424-765-4 (UK)
ISBN-13: 978-0-8254-6131-6 USA)
ISBN-10: 0-8254-6131-6 (USA)

Distributed by:
UK: Marston Book Services Ltd, PO Box 269,
Abingdon, Oxon OX14 4YN;
USA: Kregel Publications, PO Box 2607,
Grand Rapids, Michigan 49501.

The text paper used in this book has been made from
wood independently certified as having come from
sustainable forests.

British Library Cataloguing Data
A catalogue record for this book is available from
the British Library.

Printed and bound in Malta by Gutenberg Press.

Contents

Introduction

William Wilberforce:
A Man Of Courage, Commitment and Mission –
But A Mission Not Yet Complete

"William Wilberforce": the name rightly reminds us of a courageous and dedicated man who fought with determination against fierce opposition, rooted in many vested interests, to end Britain's involvement in the infamous slave trade.

During his early years in Yorkshire he showed few signs of the man he was to become. He was a sickly child and did not do well at school. Nevertheless, he went to St John's College, Cambridge – where he did not take his studies seriously. Here are his first impressions:

> *I was introduced on the very first night of my arrival to as licentious a set of men as can well be conceived. They drank hard, and their conversation was even worse than their lives.*

He adopted an extravagant lifestyle, and spent much of his time playing cards. However while at Cambridge he met the future prime minister, William Pitt the Younger, and formed a lasting friendship that was later to play an important role in his parliamentary career and political endeavours.

Milestones in the Life of a "Mighty Shrimp"

- In 1780 he was elected as an MP to the House of Commons for Hull, beginning a parliamentary career that would last for 53 years.
- On March 25, 1784, Wilberforce spoke in the Castle Yard at York so eloquently that the famous biographer Boswell wrote:

  > *I saw what seemed a mere shrimp mount the table; but as I listened, he grew and grew, until the shrimp became a whale.*[1]

- In 1784 he became an evangelical Christian, a step that radically changed his life and behaviour.
- In 1787, a meeting with the dedicated slavery abolitionist Thomas Clarkson had a profound effect. On Sunday October 28, 1787, William Wilberforce wrote in his diary:

  > *God Almighty has set before me two great objects, the suppression of the slave trade and the Reformation of society.*[2]

- From 1788, for the next 18 years, Wilberforce – eventually with Pitt's support – introduced anti-slavery motions every year in Parliament. These motions had very limited results because of fierce opposition from the planters in the colonies, who relied on slaves for cheap labour. He continued to fight resolutely for the abolition of the slave trade but it took 20 years for his endeavours to begin to achieve success.
- On February 22, 1807, the House of Commons voted by an overwhelming majority of 283 votes (with only 16 against) for the abolition of the slave trade. MPs gave him the greatest standing ovation ever recorded in Parliament while he sat, head in hands, overwhelmed with emotion and relief. This parliamentary

success was quickly followed by a series of active measures to end the slave trade.

- In 1809 the Royal Navy was mobilised to search ships suspected of carrying slaves – including ships flying under foreign flags.
- 1810 saw Parliament define slave trading as a felony, carrying a punishment of fourteen years' hard labour.
- In 1814, the British representative at the Congress of Vienna successfully required the abolition of the slave trade to be included in the International Treaty, which was signed by all the European powers on June 9, 1815.
- In 1825 Britain made slave trading a crime that could carry the death penalty.
- In August 1833 the British parliament took the final step of the abolition of slavery itself throughout the Empire, and the 700,000 people still held as slaves in British territories were freed.
- On the night that Wilberforce died, his supporters in the House of Commons were passing the clause in the Emancipation Act that declared all slaves free in one year and decreed that their masters would be given £20 million in compensation.

Wilberforce had devoted 53 years to this lengthy and arduous campaign, which finally resulted in success three days before he died. He celebrated the success of his endeavours with these joyful words:

Thank God that I've lived to witness the day in which England is willing to give 20 million pounds sterling for the abolition of slavery.[1]

David J. Vaughan in his biography of Wilberforce[5] concludes with a summary of his characteristics as a model to inspire all who hold positions of leadership today, which is set out below.

- **The importance of his Christian faith:**

  Everything he was as a person, and everything he accomplished as a leader, was an expression of his Christian faith. And any attempt to "secularize" the abolition movement in Britain is a revision of history... Those immortal words penned in his diary say it all: "God Almighty has set before me..." Wilberforce believed that God had called him to the task of abolition, and it was this Christian conviction that sustained him during the long and arduous struggle (p. 300).

- **Integrity:** Wilberforce manifestly "integrated" his faith with his politics, infusing his political activities with values derived from his Christian beliefs.
- **Principled politics** – in the sense that his political activities were motivated by principles which transcended the personal and the purely political:

  A statesman who was tenacious in his pursuit of justice, indefatigable in his work for charity, and, most important, impervious to the corruption of power or fame (p. 307).

- **Realism:** He was committed to the achievement of practical results; he was a reformer, not a revolutionary. He was deeply disturbed by the French Revolution and the ways in which revolutionary zeal could unleash the destructive forces that led so many to their death at the guillotine.
- **Political activism motivated by compassion:** History is replete with examples of reformers so passionate and motivated by "righteous indignation" that they become embittered and prone to hatred. Not only the French Revolution but also many others, such as revolutions in the name of Communism, have resulted in the sacrifice of millions of people on the altars of

ideology. Although Wilberforce was deeply angered by the horrors of the slave trade, and the politics of injustice which sustained it, he never allowed his indignation to turn into hatred of people.

- **Undaunted perseverance** was a major factor in his eventual success. There are those who argue that slavery would have been abolished in time, or would have "died out" because of social and economic factors such as industrialization. But, as Vaughan rightly argues, the historical fact is this: abolition and emancipation throughout the British Empire took place when it did because of the perseverance of William Wilberforce and his supporters.

> *He fought an upward battle against powerful and hostile opposition; he was not riding along on a pleasant wave of historical necessity... A sentence from Swift's epitaph speaks poignantly of Wilberforce: "Imitate him if you can; he served the cause of human liberty (pp. 309–10).*

There is now a great need for others to imitate him. For in 2007, when we celebrate his achievements, we cannot celebrate the end of slavery. Instead, we must be challenged by the continuing existence of this dehumanising practice and we need to mark this year of commemoration with a determination to eradicate slavery from the face of the earth.

It was as long ago as 1927 that the International Slavery Convention outlawed slavery worldwide. Article 2 requires member states to take the necessary steps to bring about, progressively and as soon as possible, the complete abolition of slavery in all its forms. But, today, 80 years later, more people are enslaved than at any time in history: 27 million is one conservative estimate. So Wilberforce's mission to abolish slavery is far from accomplished, and it is our shame that millions of people are still suffering some form of slavery today.

International protest and systematic actions ranging

from economic sanctions and boycotts to political and religious rallies succeeded in bringing an end to one form of injustice – apartheid. So why are we, as individuals, as political
parties, as churches, or as the "international community", so
half-hearted in our endeavours to end the practice of slavery,
which is at least as brutal in its violations of fundamental
human rights as was apartheid?

Because pictures and personal accounts often speak
louder than statistics, in this book we will focus on three notorious examples of countries where we can witness the horrors
of modern slavery in poignant detail, with first-hand accounts
from those who have been enslaved. Our case studies come
from Sudan, northern Uganda and Burma (Myanmar). Many
are based on personal encounters with those who have been
enslaved as victims of the brutal policies of oppressive
regimes. Then we will review the history of slavery and survey
the current disturbing situation, identifying different forms of
contemporary slavery in various countries.

Slavery is a blight on the face of the earth and we in our
generation should strive to achieve, belatedly, the successful
completion of the 1927 Slavery Convention's commitment to
eradicate it in all its forms. Therefore, it is our hope that this
book, which documents the continuation of this barbaric practice, will stimulate more effective action to ensure that William
Wilberforce's valiant endeavours do not remain unfulfilled and
that the year of the commemoration of his achievements is not
a year of condemnation of our failures.

PART ONE

Modern Slavery: The Voices of Today's Slaves

Introduction

The statistics of modern-day slavery are shocking – and a challenge to us all. But behind each statistic is a human being – a man, woman or child; and behind each human being is a family and a community, which have been devastated or destroyed by the horror of slavery in our world today.

As real-life experiences often speak louder than objective, academic descriptions, we shall introduce some of the hundreds of people whom one of the authors has met personally. Great care has been taken to ensure the validity and authenticity of the evidence obtained.

We have selected three areas where Caroline Cox has had the opportunity to interview people who have endured the horror and the humiliation of enslavement in some form: chattel slavery in Sudan; forced labour and sexual slavery in Burma, and abduction of children as child soldiers both in Burma and in Uganda.

The people whose stories we record here are the "lucky" ones, in that they have escaped and made their way back to their homelands or to freedom elsewhere. However, even after their escape, the nightmares remain and the aftermath of slavery blights their lives. For example, they often find that their families have perished; their homes may have been destroyed. Girls or young women who have been abducted may find it very hard to attract a "good" husband, as they will have been forced into sexual relationships. Women returning with babies conceived through sexual relations with their masters may find that their children are not welcomed by the local community. And, for all, there is the memory of their ordeal and the stigma of having been a slave.

SUDAN

Source: Central Intelligence Agency

CHAPTER ONE

Let the Slaves of Sudan Speak

Introduction

Sudan, like many African countries, has some traditions of slavery. Inter-tribal conflicts were often associated with raids in competition for land and livestock. In some of those raids, people, especially women and children, might be abducted as slaves. But this type of slavery was not a systematic policy, sponsored and resourced by a national or local government.

Much more widespread and systematic was the massive enslavement of Africans by Arabs, in which, for more than a thousand years, many millions of Africans were captured and enslaved by Arabs. It has been estimated that Arabs enslaved more Africans than were enslaved in the whole of the notorious and well-documented Atlantic slave trade.

The traditional practices of slavery were eventually discouraged under colonial rule. But Arab enslavement of Africans began to recur in Sudan after independence. It gathered some momentum in the 1980s, and then escalated with the specific encouragement of slavery as a weapon of war by the Islamist National Islamic Front (NIF) regime.

The NIF seized power by military coup in 1989 to become the "Government of Sudan", and quickly declared militaristic Islamic jihad against all who opposed it – Muslims in opposition as well as Christians and traditional believers. As had been the case over the centuries, one of the weapons of jihad was slavery, especially of women and children. In a typical raid, men would generally be killed and the women and children taken away as slaves. They could then be exploited in ways that would fulfil the NIF's objectives: the forced Islamisation of those not already Muslims; and the forced Arabisation of the African peoples of the South and other regions ranging from Abyie in the west to the Nuba Mountains.

We record here the stories of some of the people Caroline Cox has met during many visits to Sudan in the 1990s.[1] Great care was taken to ensure as much reliability and validity of the data obtained from the interviews as possible, including cross-checking of evidence from different sources, independent selection of interviewees by random sampling and, in many cases, double-checking translations from the local African languages or from Arabic. Also, in many cases, visible evidence of physical scarring was checked to match accounts of torture, beating or other forms of reported mal-treatment.

On several visits, independent representatives of the media (television and newspapers) accompanied our groups. Generally, they embarked on each visit with appropriate scep-ticism about the existence of slavery and sometimes with hos-tility to the concept of redemption. In my experience, on almost every visit, they returned convinced by the reality of slavery and sympathetic to the policy of freeing those for whom it was possible to negotiate their release.[2]

Slavery in North-western Bahr el-Ghazal

Nyamllel, Sokobat, Majok Kuom and Manyiel.

Nyamllel is a town in an area inhabited by the Dinka tribe. It is situated in very lush, green terrain bordering the river Lol, a tributary of the White Nile. It had clearly been a flourishing township, with a market and several well-constructed red-brick buildings, including a Roman Catholic church, a clinic, and schools for boys and girls. Two priests and a number of NGOs (non-governmental organisations) had been working there, until everything changed on the fateful day of March 25, 1995. A horde of troops including murahaleen (local tribesmen from the north, backed and armed by the NIF), "Government of Sudan" (GOS) army soldiers and Popular Defence Force (PDF) mujahidin (jihad warriors) swept into the town and surrounding area, killing 82 men and capturing 282 women and children as slaves. They looted all possessions and livestock, burnt or destroyed brick buildings and tukuls, and left a trail of devastation and suffering.

The priests escaped and the NGOs withdrew, because the place was clearly a high security risk and the "Government of Sudan" had removed Nyamllel from the list of "approved" landing strips and locations for international aid agencies. The remaining local people were thus totally bereft of aid, with family members killed or taken as slaves – many of those left behind had been tortured by the enemy during the attack, and were left without medicines or any personal possessions and livestock.

Briefing by local community leaders on DATE

Having set up camp under a mango tree by the devastated clinic, we met the local civil administrators:

- Garang Amok Mou, area secretary for the local relief association;
- Garang Lual Atak, local council administrator;
- Joseph Akok Akol, executive director of Awiel West County.

They reported that slavery had become very widespread. Garang Amok Mou had himself lost seven brothers in one attack by Arabs – four had been killed and three taken alive.

> *The family tried to rescue them, but they were defeated by*
> *'the system'. The enemy were armed to the teeth by the*
> *GOS. We were armed with spears and they were armed*
> *with Kalashnikovs. My brothers were killed because they*
> *were holding spears to try to defend their family and they*
> *were mown down by automatic rifles.* (Reference needed?)

The local leaders argued that slavery was used to debilitate and exhaust the Christian communities; civilians were enslaved or forcibly dispersed; they had to surrender and submit to becoming Muslims or they would be killed. This forms part of a policy on Arabisation and Islamisation: the community leaders argued that the "Islamic League" has given money to Sudan to open a route for Islam to go deep into Africa. Southern Sudan and the Nuba Mountains are the gateway. Turabi's[3] policy is designed to capture Africa for Islam:

> *They are determined; they don't have ears to hear or to lis-*
> *ten to the international community. They are fundamen-*
> *talists and don't listen to anyone. They don't even mind*
> *being killed because, according to the Koran, if they are*
> *fighting a holy war, they will go to heaven.*

Another community leader added his account of the situation. Referring to a recent raid by the PDF on the neighbouring village of Chelkou, he said that the final toll of dead and injured civilians was still not known. He also pointed out that the Commissioner, our host at Nyamllel, would be personally very worried, as Chelkou was his home village:

> *For the Commissioner, these are his own people; they are*
> *not numbers, but names. Some of the dead or wounded*
> *may even be his own children.*

He then described how the PDF militia operate:

> *They come and kill us because we are not Muslims. They*
> *believe that if they die they will go straight to heaven,*
> *because they are fighting infidels. If they find small boys,*

they take them and force them to become Muslims; if they find older boys or men, they kill them. They have no idea of human rights. We do what we can. But this is different from traditional inter-tribal conflicts, because of the involvement of the GOS – arming, training and encouraging the PDF. There is also an ideological, religious dimension of forced Islamisation.

During many visits to this region, we would walk from Nyamllel to other villages such as Sokobat, two hours away, crossing the river Lol by canoe and wading through two other smaller rivers; or to Manyiel (three hours' walk). All had suffered the same fate as Nyamllel. Wherever we went we would find the people still anguished by the loss of relatives killed or captured and by the aftermath of looting and pillaging by Arab raiders. We were introduced to local people whose stories illustrate the tragedy of these recent events.

In Sokobat, the local chief gave the background to their problems. On January 2, 1995 the village of Wud Arul, about 2km north of Sokobat, was attacked. Arab raiders came at dawn, storming through the whole area, looting and burning homes to ashes, kidnapping women and children (even babies), killing old men and women. About 150–200 men came, some on horseback, some on foot, and took away 63 women and children, as well as 400 head of cattle. The women and children were taken via Um Ajac to either Meyram or Abu Jabra. There the captives were divided up and sent to the market – some to be used for forced labour in agricultural work with groundnuts or sesame; young women to become concubines; older women to become domestic slaves.

The chief explained the motives behind these raids: they were inspired by the GOS who wished to destroy the economy and the livelihood of the people of southern Sudan. To do so, they mobilised and armed local Arab tribesmen (murahaleen), who were encouraged to take wealth from the south. But the hidden agenda is to destroy the Africans in the south.

The human agony: The stories of the slaves

These testimonies were taken over a series of visits. They are not presented in chronogical order.

Enslaved families

(i) The Apin Apin Akot family, consisting of husband, wife and three children. The wife, Acai Ancook Barjok, was captured with two of the children – Afaar Apin Apin (aged approx. four years) and Akel Apin Apin (aged nine years). According to Acai Ancook Barjok:

> The Arabs came at dawn and captured us; on the way they "did what they wanted with us". They tied babies onto horses and our daughter has a paralysed leg as a result. We walked on foot for two days. We were taken to Meyram to a camp, where they built a fence around us, and kept us there. We were beaten every day, any time they felt like it. They took the girls to work. I was there for three-and-a-half months. They took some of the girls and women to Amar – a place where slaves are traded with a camel-owning tribe. I don't know what happened to them. I was lucky not to be taken there. Sometimes we had to work as domestic slaves or as water carriers. I had to work in the home of a man called Nuwer Omer. For food, we were only given unground sorghum – no milk, no oil, nothing else. This man had five slave children. He still has one of our children – a daughter aged nine, called Akel Apin Apin, because my husband did not have enough money to pay for her release. My husband, Apin Apin Akot, managed, at considerable risk of being caught and tortured, to obtain concrete information about where we were. He paid an Arab informer (name supplied but not published here, to protect sources) a bribe of £50,000 (Sudanese) for the information and he took him to the man who was keeping his children. He asked for the release of all his family, but the owner said that the £100,000 (Sudanese) – the

equivalent of 25 cows – which was all he had managed to collect, was not enough and he therefore kept our elder daughter, until her father could raise another £50,000 (Sudanese).

Mr Apin Apin Akot had to walk for six days to reach Meyram and for a further day to find his family at Dhelim, where slaves were kept, out of sight of the authorities. He said that he saw "many, many" slaves in Dhelim.

When the husband and wife had finished recounting their tragic story, they wept at the thought of the plight of the daughter they had had to leave behind: as she was nearly old enough to be "married", she would be circumcised and forcibly betrothed to an Arab. Despite their manifest grief, the father said with great graciousness:

We are grateful that you have taken the trouble to come here to see this tragedy and we hope your words describing our grief will go around the world.

Before leaving, we gave Mr Apin Apin Akot and his wife the money he would need to buy the freedom of their elder daughter and were rewarded with radiant smiles of relief. On a subsequent visit, Mr Apin Apin Akot came running to meet us, his face wreathed with smiles, exclaiming excitedly:

I'm so happy, I rescued my elder daughter just in time. Every morning, I wake up a happy man and I praise God, because we are together again as a family.

(See photo section.)

(ii) A woman called Abol Wol Angara had lost all her four children, who had been taken into slavery: Deng Ayoom aged 21, Abuk Ayoom Ayoom (18), Nalow Ayoom Ayoom (16) and Agor Ayoom Ayoom (14). They are all in captivity and she has no idea of their whereabouts. Her husband is dead and she has no one to help her to get her children back again.

(iii) Aluiat Majok, a young mother, together with a baby son (Bikit Osman) conceived during sexual relationships imposed by her master. She had been kidnapped during a raid in 1988 and described her experiences thus:

> *When the Arab militia came, their first target was the cat-*
> *tle but they also abducted many people, killing any who*
> *resisted and concentrating mainly on women and chil-*
> *dren. My master took two boys as well as me; I tried to*
> *escape but was beaten, so I surrendered. They came on*
> *horseback. My master's name is Osman Issa; the two boys*
> *who were captured with me are still there.*

She then gave further details of her experiences: she had been taken to her master's home in the village of Abu Jabra, where she had been used as a domestic servant, pounding dura and collecting firewood; but when her master's wife went out to the market, she was summoned to his room and *"he took advantage of me".*

She was very lonely, being ignored by the family and eating alone whatever they chose to give her. She had to learn Arabic and adopt Muslim practices. She was given the Muslim name of Fatima and complied with Muslim practices out of fear, although she did not want to participate in these practices.

She tried to escape twice, but was caught and severely beaten. When her master's wife found she was pregnant and saw the baby, she asked her how she had become pregnant. When Aluiat Majok said that it was her master who was the father, his wife became very angry and tried to get her out of the house. In this way she managed to establish contact with one of the Arab traders, who brought her and her baby back to the south, selling them to her family for five cows.

Now, she has been welcomed warmly by her family, but, having had sexual relations with her Arab master, she will not be able to marry a young Dinka husband. As many men have been killed, she may find an old man who will be willing to marry her – but any prospects of a "normal" marriage are hopelessly blighted.

(iv) Aker Deng, a girl aged approximately fourteen, was captured with another girl by Mohammed Edber in 1988. They were beaten and forced to look after cattle. She stayed in her master's house and, if ever anything was lost, she was blamed and was beaten by her master or his son, Ibrahim. She was not given clothes, only rags, and was fed on sorghum, which was not always "properly washed". She was called by an Arabic name, Naima, and required to go to the mosque; if she refused, she was beaten. She said that she did often refuse and was always beaten. She was brought back in March 1995 and her brother paid five cows for her freedom – two of which were owned by the family and the rest given by other people.[4]

(v) A young blind mother, Abuk Marou Keer, whose two sons had been taken as slaves to the north: Abuk Deng, aged seven and Deng Deng, aged five. They had been captured during the raid on Nyamllel in March 1995. She had been told by the Arab traders that the boys were alive and that their whereabouts were known. They were owned by a man called Omar who lived at a village called Bethek, near Muglad. She was desperate, saying:

> In Africa, if you are blind, your children are your eyes. I am blind and I have lost my children. I don't know what I will do. I will die.

As she had lost everything in the raid and had no means of raising the money for the redemption of her boys, the local civil authorities asked if we could help her. When we provided the necessary money, she said:

> When I get the money, we will start to retrieve the children within five days. We will pound dura and cook food for the journey. My brother and sister will go to bring my children back.

On a subsequent visit a few months later, we visited Abuk Marou Keer in her compound and found a radiantly happy young mother, smiling broadly and exclaiming:

> *I'm so happy! I have my children again. I'm so happy, I could dance – except I can't dance because I'm blind. But that doesn't matter. At least we are together again as a family* (See photo sectiion.)

(vi) A man, Atur Jong Mawien, from the village of Majok Kuom, which was raided the previous day. His wife and children were captured by the PDF during a previous raid in April 1994. He had worked very hard to raise money to buy back his wife, son and two daughters. When he had sufficient means to redeem them he started to walk along the border to try to find his family. He located his children scattered in different villages. But when he was at Muglad he was caught by the PDF. They tortured him, tying his wrists and ankles together, hanging him from a beam and beating him. He was then unconscious for three days. He said he saw many fellow prisoners die. He was accused of being an agent of the SPLA (Sudanese People's Liberation Army).[5] Then a senior PDF officer arrived from El Obeid. He was a "decent" man and ordered the local PDF jailers to stop maltreating the prisoners. He was released, but was so badly injured he could not walk. The senior PDF officer said he had suffered so much that his children should be released without payment, and arranged for this to be done. He concluded: *"God was with me. I just wanted to come to give you my story."*

He had brought his wife, son and two daughters with him. However, he still has two other sons in captivity and is deeply worried that he is now so disabled by his maltreatment that he cannot work to raise the money for their release.

(vii) Majok Majok was in his home in Nyamllel when the raid occurred in March 1995. The PDF surrounded his house, capturing his wife and sons. They were taken to Muglad, four days' walk away. There, the family was split up. One son was taken to a cattle camp but managed to escape. Majok Majok then raised money for those members of the family still enslaved and managed to make the journey to Muglad. He happened to see his other son in the market and managed to persuade the owner to sell him back for £37,000 Sudanese pounds. His wife, when she was a slave, was forced to carry water and managed to escape on the way back from the bore-hole. Three days ago they were all reunited back at home.

> *Then, yesterday, our village suffered another raid. But we heard the sound of guns and ran as fast as we could to Sokobat. We managed to escape, but others didn't. We just came here because we heard you were here and we wanted to tell you our story. Now we will go back.*

(viii) Kuei Kiir Deng, a woman aged 26:

> *"On 3rd March 1995 my husband and I were by the river in Nyal Chor. Suddenly government soldiers, who were riding on horseback, attacked us. They shot my husband dead and they gouged my eye out. They tied my hands together and tied me to a horse and forced me to go north with them. I was not given any food and the journey was very difficult. There were thorns along the path and my skin was cut as I walked.*
>
> *I was taken to El Muglad to stay with a slave owner called Mohammed and his two wives. They did very bad things to me. They would beat me if I refused to do any-thing that they said and I had to work whenever they told me. The slave owner forced me to have sex with him whenever he wanted. If I tried to refuse, he would beat me. I have an eight-month-old baby from him. For three years I have been subjected to his continual sexual abuse. I have just managed to get here three days ago. It has been a very hard time but I have to tell you what happened to me because it is not right to hide these things and people must know what is happening.*

(ix) Achang Mayol, a women, 27 years old:

> *I and my three children – Nyayh Chan, a seven-year-old girl; Kuol Chan, a five-year-old boy; and a baby girl, one1-year-old Achai Chan – were captured in 1996. We heard the raiders coming with guns and artillery and tried to run away but we were surrounded and captured. The children were put on donkeys or horses and the women were tied together by ropes and dragged along because they were on foot. We had to walk for twelve days with very little food and we drank water from the rivers when we could get it. We were beaten when we walked slowly. We had to spend the nights in makeshift compounds where we were surrounded by armed soldiers. We eventually reached Setep where I became a slave to Mohammed Abdullah and his wife. I had to cultivate crops and my children were required to look after the goats. We were given just two cups of sorghum to last for seven days, occasionally complemented by some okra. I had to live with Mohammed Abdullah, who was one of the murahaleen taking part in the raids. Eventually traders came and took me back. When we returned we found that there was nothing left. Everything had been destroyed. We are very poor and we have nothing with which to buy our freedom.*

(x) Abuk Adour, a woman, aged about 25:

> *During the fighting in a raid on my village of Achok in 1997 I and my children, Ayul Arop, a seven-year-old boy; Deng Arop, a five-year-old boy; and two daughters, Nykiir and Nikat Arop, aged four and three, were captured and taken north. I had to work in the house of my owner, Oman Jama, while my children were sent to a separate village near Goth to look after goats and cattle. I have tried to look for my children but could not find them. When the chance came for freedom, I decided that I had to take it and not risk delay in case I was detained. I am profoundly sad being separated from my children. It is absolutely*

terrible to have to be away from my children.
very tough. I am so unhappy that I do not eve
with my husband or to have relationship
because I am grieving for the loss of my child. ....

(xi) Mayen Anyang, a 52-year-old man:

I was at the market in Abin Dau with my two wives,
Aman (35) and Nyanud (28), and our five children,
Mangok (male, 16), Nyadeing (female, 15), Aguek (female,
15), Mangok (male, 5) and Nyivol (female, 3) when the
raiders came. We were all taken captive. I was tied by my
wrists in a chain to other captives. The journey to the
north was very hard. We had to walk for about two solid
days. We were given scarcely any food and I, and my chil-
dren, were beaten. I have a scar on my wrist from where I
was bound. At the end of my journey I was separated from
my family and taken to a camp in Shetep, where I was
held for three months. There were approximately 400 men
in the camp. My hands and my legs were tied. Those who
ran the camp put constant pressure on me to convert to
Islam. About twice a day they would tell me that I should
convert. They told me that we should all become Muslim
and then it would be possible to live together as brothers,
but that if we did not they would kill us all. They also said
they were punishing us because my people had tried to kill
their people. However, most of the pressure focused on try-
ing to make me convert to Islam. On several occasions
this was accompanied by beatings. About a week after my
arrival I was beaten severely with sticks. The upper bone
in my arm now sticks out as a result of this beating. On
another occasion, during the night, they came to me again
and told me that I must become a Muslim and that they
would beat me if I did not. I cannot change my religion. I
am a Christian and have committed myself to Christ. I
cannot change my belief. As I would not comply with their
commands, they attacked me, stamping on my chest. I

was nearly paralysed. After five days I still could not stand up or use my legs or my hands properly. I have a visible scar on my chest from that attack. I am still suffering with pain in my back, along my spine and in my chest and my hips. There are people in the north who are not against us but are sympathetic to us. They came and talked to me and told me that everyone is born to be free. They paid money for me and brought me back to the south. I am so happy to be back here. However, the famine is here now and the hunger is much worse than when I went away. My greatest difficulty is that my whole body is in pain. Also, my wife and my five children are still in the north. However, seeing you here gladdens my heart. Those who secured my freedom are like the hand of God reaching out to save me.

(xii) Marol Mai, a 42-year-old man:

My home has been destroyed by northern raiders three times since 1993. In that year I was living in Agok. Soldiers and Arab merchants on horses, camels and foot descended on us. They took my entire herd of livestock, which was 32 cows. They burnt my home and took absolutely everything I possessed. I could not save anything. They took my daughter, Abul Marol, who was ten years old at the time. She is still in captivity in Shetep.

I ran away from the area and went with my family to Mayen Abun, where we tried to rebuild our lives, and I built two huts there. However, in 1995 we were again attacked by raiders. They came on horseback and on foot and had guns. They entered my house and chased me away. Then they set fire to my house and to all my property. They took my sons Bol (10, also present), Maluk (8) and Deng (5).

After this raid, I was again left with nothing. I left Mayen Abun and went to live in Achan. However, in April this year the raiders came again. They burnt my hut and took the little livestock I had managed to accumulate in this time, which was a meagre two cows. They beat my wife, Ngol (30). She is still in pain and I believe she may have suffered broken ribs from the attack. They killed two of my children, Abuk (15) and Acol (8). Seven soldiers took me by force from my hut. They beat me and bound my wrists. They told me that they wanted to train me to be a Muslim like them. I was tied in a chain of captives and the rope was attached to a horse at the front. I was taken to Shetep. I was given the name Mohammed and told not to think about my family any more because I was no longer one of them. I was taken by a slave master called Ibrahim Mohammed. He had three wives and eight children. He treated me very badly. He beat me and shamed me, telling me that I was like a dog. I had to sleep outside. I was given agricultural work to do and had to work from morning to sunset. I was told that I should become a Muslim. I can't convert to Islam. Christianity is my chosen religion so I don't want to change my beliefs. They took me to the mosque, but I was allowed to stay outside. It was difficult for them to convert me because I could not understand Arabic. They beat me with sticks, seven times altogether, because I wouldn't convert to Islam and didn't learn Arabic and because they wanted to force me to work harder.

I am very happy to be back home. I feel much safer and more secure and I am relieved that I can be free. I would like to say thank you to those who have come to liberate me from slavery and who have made it possible for me to be freed. Your presence here is important, and knowing that what has happened to me can be made known makes me feel more positive about my future. Please tell people around the world that we need their help. We are in need of many things, including clothes and other material assistance.

(xiii) Achen Blual, a girl aged about twelve or thirteen:

> *I was taken in the May raid. My mother was killed in the raid and my brother and sister were also taken. I don't know where they are. My father was captured. I don't know whether he is still alive. The raiders came by horse and tied my hands and pulled me behind them. It was 30 days' footing (walk) and I was very frightened. I knew that they killed people. I was taken to Cedep with others from Abin Dau. My master had several concubines* (Achen became a little nervous at this point and we did not pursue this line of questioning). *His sons beat me and mistreated me. I washed clothes and went to the market as well as cracking the groundnuts and planting seeds. I slept outside, and if it rained I slept under sacks in the corner. I escaped after four months and a trader found me and brought me back here. I am so happy to be free. I am going to live with my relatives in Abin Dau.*

(xiv) Kuot Tholong, a 70-year-old man:

> *I was taken from my home village of Gumgoi in April 1996. I heard the raiders coming and I hid in the grass, but the raiders set the grass on fire. Two men either side of me were killed but I was beaten up and taken. We were in a long line behind them – many women and children as well as some men. I was taken to Nabaga and told to tend the cattle and cultivate. I was given the husks of millet and sorghum remains to eat. My master, Kubri Ahmed, had three other male slaves, one was beaten and taken to hospital – and two women slaves in their twenties. I could hear the women crying out at night when they were raped. I slept nearby under a tree.*
>
> *I was called Gara (Pumpkin). They treated me badly and beat me* (He showed us a bone jutting out from his wrist). *They made me crouch on a fire grate, burning my testicles. When I complained they just laughed at me. I*

escaped by night and met another person who found a local Dinka who knew a trader.

(xv) A 28-year-old mother, Mary Juac Deng, and her three children Regina (3), Anjelina (6) and Tereza (8):

We were captured when Regina was still breast feeding. This was ten miles away in Acuanac. My husband was away when the raiders came. I was taken to Bahri outside Khartoum and our master was Khalid Salah. I was kept in his house. My children were put in an Arabic school and given new names, Halima, Nesera and Kadija, which made them sad. I served in the house and my girls helped me with washing the dishes. My master was an old man. I slept in the kitchen with the children. Regina knows only Arabic now. We escaped at night and came down by lorry to Abyei. My husband is very happy that we are back.

(xvi) Akuac Mathiane, a woman about 34 years old:

In May 1998 Sudanese Popular Defence Forces, together with murahaleen, came on horseback and attacked my village, Aweng (Bahr el-Ghazal). They killed many people, mainly men, including my brother and my nephew. Some of those killed were fighting the forces but many were unarmed civilians. I was taken captive with two of my three children and a large number of other women and children. My captors snatched my two-year-old son, Mayai, from me and threw him harshly onto the ground. He still has a scar on his chest from where he was hurt as he was thrown down on to a sharp object.

Our wrists were tied and we were tied to horses. The children were placed on the horses and we were forced to walk for ten days to the north. We were told that all the people in the village would be killed. We were given very little sustenance, just dura mixed with sand and water that had been polluted with urine. This was deliberately done to show the raiders' contempt for us. One of the children died on the way, from hunger. I and the other women were sexually abused during the trip to the north.

I was taken to Kitep near Goth in western Sudan, where I was kept by the man who had captured me in the raid. His name is Feki and I lived with him and his wife, who both mistreated me. There were five of us who had been taken as slaves who were kept in his household. My children were taken away from me and given to someone else.

I was completely distraught; I did not know what to do; I did not know where my children were and I did not know whether my husband and my five-year-old daughter, Ajak, who had not been taken north, were still alive. I felt overwhelmed and completely helpless.

I was made to work, cooking and cultivating dura. I had to work from dawn for long hours and was given very little food. Only when I became weak would they give me a little food. I had to sleep outside. The children were treated better because it was intended that they would be adopted. I and the other women in slavery with me were sexually abused during our captivity. I was given an Arabic name, Amila, and Mayai was given the name Mohammed.

I am an animist, but I was forced to pray like a Muslim. They told me that since I was their slave I had to do what they said, and when I refused to pray they would beat me with sticks. This happened almost daily.

They called us names and told us that Dinkas were worthless and only the northerners were of value. They said that we deserved only poor food and care and that we were supposed to be killed. I was told that I had been taken as a slave because they were fighting with the Dinkas. I think that the primary motivation of the fighting is that they want the land and the secondary motivation is that they want to force us to adopt Islam.

My brother raised some money to try to buy me back from the owner. However, he was told that it was not enough. He increased the amount and I managed to escape. I had to hide during the day on the way down to the south. It took us fifteen nights to travel back. I arrived about two months ago.

My brother managed to find my youngest son as well and he is now with me. My six-year-old son, Daw, and my three sisters, Abuk, aged eight, Diu, aged seven, and Nyariak, aged six, are all still in the north. I am unable to get them back because we do not have enough money because all our livestock was taken in the raid. I would be able to trace my son; I just do not have enough money to get him when I find him.

I am very happy to be back and to find that there are people still alive after the raid. However, everything that I had was taken in the raid and I am uncertain about the future and do not know how I will live. I am very badly affected by my experiences. I am very afraid for my son who is still in captivity and I cannot sleep at night because I am worrying about him. I also live in fear that the raiders will return.

On one visit to Nyamllel, we set off for the village of Majok Kuom, beyond Sokobat, approximately four hours' walk from Nyamllel. We began by riding bicycles, but the abundance of thorn bushes took their toll of tyres and, after numerous puncture repairs, we completed the journey on foot.

This village had just suffered a raid by PDF forces accompanying the train from Wau to El Obeid, and we wanted to obtain evidence of what had happened. On arrival, we were confronted by a desolate scene of burnt tukuls and charred rubble. Nothing was left intact. All harvested crops were burnt. No livestock were left. We were told that twelve women and children had been captured and taken as slaves; three had escaped but nine were still missing.

We spoke to two survivors:

(i) Tong Anei was in his hut when a group of eight armed militia surrounded him. He was taken to a tree, where he was beaten and held while his wife and daughter, aged fifteen, were abducted in front of his eyes. He witnessed children being rounded up and tied together. Women who were abducted were beaten and forced to carry their captors' loot of dura and groundnuts on their heads. When the enemy had taken all the possessions they could carry, they burnt everything else that remained. They took all the livestock.

> *I had eleven sheep, 21 goats, and four cows. They are all gone. Even my clothes have been taken. So I am left alone without anything – even food. My hut with all its contents, which they did not take away, was burnt. Many people ran away when they heard the soldiers coming, but I stayed to try to protect my wife and daughter. When they came, they were shouting "Allah Akhbar; Allah Akhbar". They took twelve people: four girls, two women and three boys. Now I am completely alone. I have no hope of getting my wife and daughter back. Last year, when we were raided, some people lost their children but were able to buy them back with cattle. But I have no capacity for this. All my livestock are gone. I have no hope of seeing them again.*

(ii) Arek Mawien (see photo section), an elderly woman who was standing in the middle of the remains of her compound, which had been reduced to piles of charred rubble. She described the events of that fateful day:

> *I was working in my home when three groups of armed soldiers came from three directions, shouting "Allah Akhbar". I was here with my two children, Anyat aged thirteen and Deng aged fifteen. They beat me and told me to "sit still", saying that if anyone tried to run away, they would shoot them. Two armed men threatened me with guns while they took my children away. Last year they took my cows. Now they have taken my few goats. I am left with nothing. They have burnt my home and my food;*

I do not even have any cooking pots or containers to collect water from the borehole. I am too weak to rebuild. I do not know how I shall survive.

As we left she said, with great graciousness and a courageous smile:

Thank you for coming. You are the first people to come here. You really care; thank you.

Boy slaves

(i) Angok Long, age unknown, told us:

I was kidnapped by enemy militia four years ago, while looking after cattle. My owner, named Kabush, changed my name to "Ali" and tried to force me to be a Muslim. But I refused to accept this. I was often beaten badly with a big stick because of my resistance. An Arab trader brought me back to Manyiel one month ago. I never thought I would come back home.

We witnessed the emotional reunion of Angok Long with his father.

(ii) Duang Luol, aged seven, from Manyiel was very small when he was captured and taken to Goth. He had been beaten, and showed us scars on his head and both legs. He said he was given only basic grain, sometimes chaff, for food. He had not been called by his own name, but "Miskeen". He was very unhappy because he had come home, but he had not been able to see his parents – his mother was a long way away and his father was at the front line fighting for the SPLA.

(iii) Bop Thomg, from Manyiel, had been captured two years ago and taken to a place near Ed Dain. His master's name was Muman. He had to look after goats. He was given millet, chaff and sometimes "porridge" to eat. He had to work all day, every day, from morning until night. He was given a Muslim name – Mohammed. He said he thought he would never be able to come home. He had seen his mother since his return, but his father had been killed while he was away in captivity. His final "message" was:

I am proud to be a Dinka boy.

(iv and v) Two boys, Bol Kuol (aged approximately thirteen), and Deng Kuol (approximately six). The older boy had been kidnapped with his mother, who was pregnant with his younger brother, who was born in captivity. The boys were given Arabic names: Amma and Mohammed. The older boy described their experiences:

They were kidnapped in 1988 from the village of Akwal Malwal during a battle. Initially he and his mother fled, but returned when they thought it was safe to do so and ran into another attack. They were kidnapped and his father was killed. The attack was carried out by Arab militia – some on horseback, others on foot. When they were caught, his mother had to walk; he was put on his master's horse. His master's name was Mohammed Issa. When they arrived in the north, they were treated like cattle, living in a cattle camp at Nubi; they were not provided with accommodation in a house – only plastic sheeting. They were forced to adopt Islamic practices, although his mother "acted stupid" and pretended she did not understand what was required of her. They also had to speak Arabic and now his Arabic is better than his Dinka; his small brother speaks only Arabic. They were frequently addressed as "Abid" (Arabic for "slaves").

They eventually managed to escape to Mutari, where they met some of the contacts of the trader "Ibrahim" (pseudonym, to protect his identity) who helped them. The price for their freedom was stipulated by "Ibrahim" as five cows or one automatic rifle for each of the two boys and their mother. Many members of their family were killed in the raid and their surviving relatives have been able to find only three cows, so they cannot be reunited until the remainder of the ransom is found. If they have to return to the north, they fear they will be killed.

(vi). Duwar Athar, Dinka boy aged six:

> *My parents were both killed in Aweng four months ago. I don't have any brothers or sisters. I am staying with Alek Mayen (Alek Mayen identified herself and said, "I already have six children. I keep him because I don't want him to die but I don't have enough food"). I was taken to Muglid and stayed with a man called Mohammed. I served naked just like I am now. I was treated very badly and I was forced to talk in Arabic or I was beaten* (he had a visible scar on his forehead). *I was called Jengai. My master had a wife and two children, who were nasty to me. I was forced to tend the cattle and I was only given scraps of food. I was very lonely and I cried every day... sometimes for my parents and sometimes because they beat me.*
>
> *I know I am going to die... I don't have any food.*

Throughout the whole interview Duwar had his eyes lowered to the ground, and the sadness never left them.

(vii) Bol Marol, 10 (see photo section).

> *I was taken as a slave in 1995 and have been in slavery for three years. I was taken by a slave master. He was tall with a dark beard and he was very aggressive towards me. I was made to look after sheep and goats and to clean dishes. I worked from about 6am to 6pm and they gave me only a little food. They would beat me with sticks to make me work harder. I have a scar on my face from one of these beatings. My slave master tried to convert me to Islam. He forced me to go to the mosque with him on Fridays and beat me with sticks to make me go. I did not want to convert to Islam because I am a Christian and do not want to change my religion. What happened to me and is happening to others like me is a very bad thing. I am happy that I can come back to my home and that I have found that*

someone cares about me and can tell others about what has happened to me.

(viii) Lual Deng, aged thirteen, from Nyamllel, had been caught in the March 1995 raid and managed to escape. But, on the way, he was caught by three Arab militia men who beat him with sticks and stabbed him in both hips with knives (wounds still visible) so that he would not be able to walk. They left him lying wounded on the ground. He managed to crawl home.

(ix) Deng (family name not known) had just returned with an Arab trader. As Caroline Cox was talking to him, he was very unhappy and traumatised. He had just learnt that both his parents had been killed in the raid in which he had been abducted two years previously. However, towards the end of the meeting, he smiled wistfully, saying: *"At least I am home again now, I am called my own name 'Deng'"* (the Dinka word that means "rain". As rain is precious, it may also indicate someone who is precious and to be cherished). He added, with feeling: *"I am glad I am no longer called 'Abd'* (the Arabic for 'slave')." (See photo section.)

The Slave Raids

(i) 50-year-old Akuac Amet:

> *I was caught in my home by the Arabs on March 25. They beat me unconscious with a big club. Now my legs are paralysed and I can only crawl. They then shot my four sons who were tending cattle and abducted my fourteen-year-old daughter, Ajak. The raiders left with all of my property. My husband died in the great famine. I am now completely destitute. The owner of this tukul is helping me to survive.*

When we revisited Akuac Amet on a later visit, we found her dying in the tukul of the woman who had given her refuge after her ordeal. This woman was called Adut Wol Ngor and she was currently caring for 62 victims of the March raid. She recalled that day in words very similar to those we heard during our previous visit:

> *The enemy came early on March 25; this woman was too old to run; so they caught her and beat her so badly it was impossible to know if she was alive or dead. The enemy returned and killed her four sons and kidnapped her daughter. She can be returned, if the money can be found – but there is no one to pay the money... I came and took care of this old lady and have looked after her...*
>
> *About 300 people were killed... the enemy divided into two groups – some on horseback, some on foot... We ran with the children to try to hide them in the long grass but they found us and drove the older children away. Any who refused to go, they killed them... Those who went were tied with a rope and pulled like cows behind horses. Some children were as little as seven years old. Some died of thirst... They were not given any water...*
>
> *The families of those who were captured are still trying to find the money to pay for their children... If they have no money, they can be told that their children are still alive, but are unable to buy them back.*

When asked by a reporter how many Arabs participated in the attack, she replied:

> *If you wanted to live, you didn't stay to count the horses... but there were several hundred.*

She also expressed gratitude to us for coming:

> *We are happy you have come to meet us, to see how we are suffering; how our children have been taken by the enemy and how we are having to live without our children... and how we have to eat fruit and grass... We are grateful to you for coming to see our situation... Thank you for coming to us... We pray that God will bring our children back to us...*

(ii) Joseph Bol, from Nyamllel:

> *On March 25 1995, GOS militia attacked and took every-*
> *one by surprise. The people scattered and fled. Those chil-*
> *dren who were unable to run fast enough were captured.*

His child, Joseph Atok, aged six, was captured and, according
to accounts from some who escaped en route, was taken with
the others to Arieth in the north. He sent his brother-in-law to
find his child. It took him a month to track down the stolen
children, in a village called Abu Simson, and his child's owner,
a man called Abul Gassim Mohammed. The master demanded
a price of five cows or the equivalent in money, but he did not
have the resources to meet these demands:

> *I have nothing. My tukul was burnt; everything I had was*
> *taken... The owner told my brother-in-law to go and find*
> *the cows and then to come back for my child. But I don't*
> *have anything or any way in which I can raise the money*
> *I need... I have no hope of being able to buy my child's*
> *freedom... I am confused and I don't know what to do.*

(iii) Akuil Garang (see photo section), a woman aged approximately 30: Two of her children were burnt alive in their hut
during the raid; when she tried to run away, she was attacked
and suffered spear and gunshot wounds; she fell down, and
they took her third child (aged six, called Atong) while she was
unconscious. One of "Ibrahim's" representatives has told her
that her child is still alive and she should find the money to go
to fetch him home. She commented:

> *But how can I ever get Atong back? I can never get the*
> *money I need to pay for him... I have nothing. We are*
> *looking for food to eat and they ask us for these impossi-*
> *ble sums of money... It is too much for me.*

(iv) Machuar Bol Akon, a man in his 30s, described how everyone tried to run away when the Arabs came, and attempted to
hide the children in long grass. But his two children (Akon

Machar Bol and Kur Machar, aged approximately six and twelve) were discovered and taken and his wife was killed. When she tried to protect them, the militia beat her to death and then took the children from her. They survived, because they ran in different directions. He had since heard that his children were alive and being kept in the north, in Meyram.

(v) Nwoon Angon, a middle-aged man, was sitting under a tree when the Arabs came and they shot him before he could escape:

> When they attacked, they didn't differentiate between men, women and children, between soldiers or civilians... They shot me and left me for dead. My children escaped, but they took all my property, livestock (30 cows) and goods and they burnt my home and my crops. I am now lame, because of my wounds, and I cannot make a living; and I have no cattle left.

(vi) Deng Deng Dong, aged twelve, speaks some English; his father was the local schoolteacher, but was killed in the raid. He described the day:

> When the militia attacked, I was with my mother and we were in front of my father. He was killed, and so was my uncle. Those who ran quickly got away; those who were slower, didn't... I lost my very best father... I can't get him back again.

The "Slave Train"

One of our visits coincided with the passage through the area of the train that travels between El Obeid in northern Sudan and the town of Wau, in the south. The train carried troops, munitions and supplies to the GOS garrison in Wau and was always accompanied by a large force of PDF troops. These militia guarded the train and fanned out into the surrounding countryside, raiding villages, killing, capturing and torturing civilians, burning homes and crops, looting and pillaging.

While we were in Nyamllel, we saw evidence of two of these raids: one on Chelkou, 22 miles south-west of Nyamllel; the other on Majok Kwam, a village four hours' walk away, which took place while we were in Nyamllel.

On arrival at Nyamllel, we were greeted with great warmth and appreciation.

Six patients needed evacuation to a hospital at Lokichokio for treatment. The aircraft that brought us in was able to take them back. The medical supplies that we brought were urgently needed, as Nyamllel was on the list of airstrips designated by the GOS as "No-Go" areas, and the people had been suffering from acute shortages of all kinds of medicine.

Very soon after our arrival, reports began to come in of the PDF raid on Chelkou. This was the home town of the Commissioner for Awiel West County, Aleu A. Jok, who was in Nyamllel during our visit. Messengers said that there had been casualties, with at least three men, one woman and one child killed (full toll not yet known); that there had been widespread destruction; that some civilians had been abducted; that the Commissioner's own home had been raided, and his belongings, including his cattle and his bicycle, had been taken. Two PDF officers also sent a letter to the Commissioner with this message:

> *In the name of God, the Merciful:*
> *Dear Outlaws,*
> *Peace be with you. We ask you to be alert, for we are coming to you at Nyamllel. Our force is 1,800 soldiers strong. We ask you to prepare yourselves for we are coming to get you at 3am – so be prepared. Be patient and courageous.*
> *El Sabur Company,*
> *El Tewakalna Company, Commander of the Forces, Captain Younis Tag-Eldin Babo.*
> *(over the page):*
> *You idiots. If you want peace, you should surrender before July, at the latest.*
> *Commander PDF Hebeid*

Hassan El-Hamer, PSE Colonel in Kordofan State.
Thank you.

In the event, the raid had been redirected to the village of Chelkou. During the following morning, the casualties were brought to Nyamllel, including a man with very extensive facial injuries. He was the village sub-chief, and had come to Chelkou when he heard the attack. The PDF were trying to capture a boy, who was running away. When the sub-chief tried to protect the boy, they shot him in the neck, the bullet passing through his mouth and causing serious trauma to the mouth and jaw. He responded well to analgesia and passed as comfortable a night as possible. A woman was also brought from Chelkou with gunshot wounds to both legs. When we contacted the ICRC (International Committee of the Red Cross) to request an emergency evacuation of the casualties, they claimed they were unable to come, because the airstrip was designated "No Go" by the NIF. We and our sponsors had to commission an emergency evacuation of the wounded to Lokichokio in Kenya for hospital treatment.

Failed Rescue Attempts

On one occasion we met two grieving fathers, who had found their enslaved children in the north, but were unable to secure their release.

i) Deng Ater Kwany from Path, near Nyamllel, recounted:

> *My wife and four children were abducted during a raid in March 1994. Three of the children and my wife managed to escape. But my eight-year-old daughter, Abuk, remained behind. She is now kept in Naykata in southern Darfur by a man named Ahmed Ahmed, who bought her from her captor. When I discovered where she was, I went north and tried to get her back by legal means. I opened a case against Ahmed Ahmed at the police station at Dira Dira, and had to pay the police 20,000 Sudanese pounds to do*

this. A police officer named Abdullah accompanied me to the home of Ahmed Ahmed. This man refused to give me my girl and demanded 50,000 Sudanese pounds for her release. The policeman said that, as Ahmed Ahmed had bought the girl from her captor, she was his property, and he could not insist on her release. I was forced to leave her there where she is badly mistreated by Ahmed Ahmed's wife, who calls her by the Muslim name Howeh... I also lost the 20,000 pounds, which the policeman refused to return to me. I had to return home empty-handed.

(ii) Den Hol from Awan said:

My thirteen-year-old boy, Awan Deng Awan, was abducted during a raid on our village in January 1995. I hired an Arab to locate my son, and he was eventually found in Faragella. I went there to get him back and found that he was owned by a man named Abdallah Mahajub Abdallah. This man has forced my boy to be a Muslim and has given him the name Ibrahim. The owner demanded 40,000 Sudanese pounds for the release of my son. Since I did not have this kind of money, I had to leave my son in captivity and return home.

Slavery in the Nuba Mountains

(i) Commander Kuwa (now deceased) was the SPLA Commander for the Nuba Mountains. He described the situation there:

The Government of Sudan is pursuing a policy of enforced assimilation of the black population in Darfur, where it is easier as they are Muslim. But in the Nuba Mountains, there are many Christians and believers in traditional religions – which is a barrier against assimilation.

When asked why he, as a Muslim, was fighting for the SPLA, he emphasised that, although he was a Muslim, he abhorred the Government of Sudan's policy of attempted enforced Islamisation. He indicated that, although he was a black African, 20 years ago he would have said he was an Arab: he attended an Islamic school, spoke Arabic better than his mother tongue, and was a Muslim. As a student he began to ask himself why his own language and culture were not recognised. He said:

> *I looked for recognition of the beauty of my Nuba land, but I never found it in Arabic poems; I looked for appreciation of the beauty of my people, and the only reference to beauty was to people with straight hair. I started to hate my own colour, my African self, my society. I started to feel this way at primary school, where the Headmaster ignored and insulted us, saying: 'Why should we teach Nuba people – they are only fit to become our servants.' At secondary school, we were told that Arab women do not work; all the domestic work is done by Nuba boys.*

(ii) Abbas Bedawi Kuku from the district of Lagawa reported:

> *In the 1980s Arab tribes were armed by the Government of Sudan and started to attack our villages. During these raids, many children were abducted. They were then sold in open markets, usually to serve their masters as shepherds. Slave markets are still functioning in Tabun, Lagawa, Al Muglad, Babanusa, and Diein. Children are usually sold for between 300 and 500 Sudanese pounds, which is about the value of two chickens or one kilo of meat. I personally knew the son of Ibrahim Tutu, who lived at Karlanya, near Tulushi. One day at the end of November 1991, the boy was watering goats when he was kidnapped during a raid by an Arab militia. He was taken away to Jangaro. Three months later, some people who knew the boy saw him there and informed his father. The*

*father went to Jangaro and bought back his son for 500
Sudanese pounds.*

*GOS troops raided many villages in the Tulushi dis-
trict at the end of November and early December 1991. I
know of fifteen people who were arrested and then taken
back to their villages, where the soldiers shot them and
burned the bodies in front of their families and neigh-
bours. They are Abdalla Kakai, Beshir Kanu, Sadan Kakki
and Biraisa Tirga from Rasel Fil; Makki Tasso Kakki, Alfes
Kuku and Mousa Kuwa from Karlanya; Ahmed Al Izeirig,
Fadl Al Nabi Al Izeing and Hisein Al Ahmar from Kamda;
and Mousa Kuku, Jodi Kuku, Ibrahim Weima and Tut
Kafi from Tulushi.*

Ismail Kafi Omdurman, from Shar Damam, near Kadugli,
described recent events:

*GOS troops attacked the village of Al Kutang at about 4
am on November 25, 1989. The women and children ran
to the caves high up in the mountains for protection.
However, the soldiers went up to the caves and shot dead
42 people. I knew a woman named Toto Musa who was
shot in the hip, but survived for one year before dying of
complications from the wound. I knew another woman
named Kiki who was shot in the knee and survived. The
captured survivors were taken to El Lihimer where the
young women were distributed among the soldiers as concubines and the children were sent to the slave market at
Lagawa. The old women were taken to the Habila agricultural project near Dilling, where they were put in camps to
perform forced labour. I knew two young women, Kaka
Tijani Tut and Kuwo Kok, who escaped and ran away to
Saraf Al Ahmar. There they were caught by soldiers who
shot them dead and then left their naked bodies by the
roadside as an example to other Nuba women. I also knew
a man named Makin whose young son had been captured
and sold into slavery. He found his son working as a*

shepherd. Makin then took a job as a shepherd to be near his enslaved son. One day, his son ran away because of his master's abuse. When the master discovered that the boy had absconded, he took the father to Kaga and murdered him. The slave owner then castrated Makim's corpse, cut off his ears and displayed the mutilated body in public to teach a lesson to disobedient slaves.

(iii) Abdul Majid Hasan from Kadugli described her fate:

I had worked as nurse in Damba, a suburb of Kadugli, since 1983. Soon afterwards the GOS started to restrict the distribution of medicine around Kadugli, believing that it would find its way into the hands of the SPLA. The Government did this by making its calculations for drug distribution on the basis of population statistics that excluded the Christian community. Then the Government decided to close all the clinics outside Kadugli and send the medical staff to Kadugli. I refused to go, and started treating people with herbs and roots because of the lack of medicine. The GOS sent out militias in 1987 to force people to leave their villages and go to Kadugli. When people refused to go, the soldiers burnt their villages to the ground. After the present regime came to power in 1989, the soldiers started to systematically destroy medical facilities and boreholes to force Nuba people to leave their villages. Many children died from smallpox, diphtheria and anaemia. In 1992, cases of kalaazar appeared in the southern part of the Nuba Mountains. We have some medical assistants still working in SPLA areas, but we have no medicine.

(iv) Rahma Kabashi from Heiban reported:

On September 10, 1985 I witnessed the torture of three people by GOS troops. The soldiers burnt the skin of three people, and then removed their finger- and toenails. Finally they drove metal nails into their heads. One of the three, Dod Codangelou, died as a result. Fifteen others were shot dead at the same time. Among them were Doud Asma of Lubi, Amur Homoda of Undurdu, Omar Garban of Hela, Abbas Mahadi of Karandal, Amur Fadal of Kigoban and Paulo Attan of Kuyani. All were accused of being members of the SPLA. I also witnessed the Sudanese army's attack on the village of Ormi on May 2, 1992. The troops burnt all the houses in the village. In one house Unan Angelou, Moussa Angelou and Doud Kalo were deliberately burnt to death. All the other men in the village were shot dead, and the women and children were taken into slavery.

The Process of Redemption

(i) By local Dinka leaders

A community leader at Naer Adut, Garang Nakuei Ken, described his involvement in trying to buy back children who had been taken into slavery. For example, during the dry season, when he was at Kiir, he met a man called Kabani Ali, who accompanied him to Abu Jabra, a town in Darfur near the Ed Daien railway (four days' walk from Kiir). They went to the home of a man called Jacob Ahmed, chief of Abu Jabra, who held 31 children captive in his house. The children had been abducted by Jacob Ahmed's tribe; they had been maltreated and had had their clothes taken away. They were denied adequate water and were so dirty that *"instead of being black, they looked green"*.

The only food they had been given was sorghum, with no salt or other food of any kind. They were very weak, some too weak to walk. The money demanded for their release was one quarter of a million Sudanese pounds, and their owner said he would not charge more *"because he was a responsible man"*.

Even so, the money was not enough to procure the release of all the children, and 16 were left behind in captivity. These were the older children, who would be more "valuable" as workers and/or as concubines. It was believed that the likelihood of their return was "very remote".

(ii) By Arab traders from the north.

(a) Discussions with a group of Arab traders selling clothes in the market near Nyamllel. Their spokesmen were Jacob Bar-el-Habib and Ali Martingale from Matarig. They said it was a six day walk in the dry season and they had to avoid checkpoints, as they would be arrested by GOS forces who would not permit such relationships with African southerners. They claimed, however, that they were *"forced to come south by famine, and need relationships with people in the south in order to survive... this is the only way we can get food and water"*.

They described the present GOS policy of encouraging attacks by Arab raiders on African southerners thus:

> *The GOS arms militias with AK47s to fight the people in the south and to act as escorts for the military trains taking supplies to Wau, to maintain GOS garrisons in the south. The militia raid villages to capture women and children and to loot whatever property they can get. There have been many raids. President Omer El Bashir and the GOS have made public the fact that they are arming these militias. On one occasion it was said on Omdurman Radio that about 3,000 had been recruited to fight the Egyptians... but many of them were sent here. So the militia are certainly armed by the GOS and encouraged to develop the slave trade.*

They also described the fate of those abducted into slavery:

> *They take the women and children to some town near the border, such as Dhayem or further north... they have to work, looking after cattle or cultivating crops or as domestic servants. For many it is a "normal life", but inevitably some are maltreated. The children don't understand what is happening but the adults are very unhappy. It is inevitable that one must pay to bring people out of captivity.*

They then described the ways in which some of those who had been abducted into slavery were brought back by Arab traders such as themselves:

> *Some colleagues bring back children and women who have been taken by force... if they find children in the north, they bring them back and sell them to their families... this is an expensive business, incurring a lot of costs, such as the provision of food and water on the journey: possibly £30,000 (Sudanese); if they are sold for £50,000 (Sudanese), the gross total is £80,000 (Sudanese).*

These Arab traders dissociated themselves from the trading of women and children for money, saying:

> *This is not a good business. It is done by bad, inhuman people. Our conscience would not allow us to deal in such business. We and the Dinkas are one people; we are brothers and we must stick together. Historically, we have always come here and had good relationships.*

(b) Discussion with another Arab trader, Eleu Atak, who helped to arrange the transactions. He claimed:

> *I am delighted to free slaves because I feel these people are my brothers.*

When asked if he had any message for his Arab brothers who captured the slaves in the first place, he replied:

> *I would tell them that taking children by force is not a good thing. People are one; we are all brothers. One should not take other people's children.*

When asked about his share of the money obtained through any transaction related to selling children back to their families, he replied:

*It all depends on how many people are involved. We have
not fixed a percentage. Soon "Ibrahinm" [the main con-
tact] will come and we will sort it all out.*

Note: The local civil authorities had to comply with the system
and not allow the complete release of returning slaves until the
full ransom was found, because they feared that, if they did not
meet these demands, the supply of women and children being
brought back from the north would be discontinued. If there
were no relatives to try to raise the ransom, the local authorities would endeavour to find resources to purchase the freedom of the women and children.

Discussion with Arab traders at Manyiel

These men often bring abducted children from the north, to
sell them back to their families. We met some of the Arab
traders and discussed the nature of their transactions. The current average price required to redeem a slave was three cows –
with a minimum of two cows. The traders claimed this price
was necessary to cover the costs of finding children, negotiat-
ing a purchase, and bringing them back.

One of these traders, C.A., explained:

*The slave owners are Arabs of the Zako tribe and also
tribes of Darfur which have been integrated into the political system of the NIF (National Islamic Front). Almost all
of them are Muslim extremists. The owners train their
slaves to be good Arabs and Muslims. A lot of slaves are to
be found in the areas around Meyram and Fashar. All the
slave raids since 1985 have been organised by the GOS.
Since we reached a peace agreement with the local Dinkas,
I have brought back more than 300 children. Just a few
days ago, I brought back twelve children. Today I brought
back 28. Some of the parents of these children will not be
able to pay the redemption fee. If the community leaders
do not come up with the fee I will not be able to bring back*

more children. This work of returning slaves is dangerous for me. But I do it because I want the Arabs and the Dinkas to live in peace.

It was estimated by the civil authorities that there were approximately 12,000 children from this area currently enslaved in the north and that the numbers were growing as raids were still continuing.

Interview with Captured Prisoner of War – A PDF Officer, Farjellah Wada Mathar, from Abu Matarik, Near Ed Daien in Darfur

He was clearly in good physical condition, appearing relaxed and on friendly terms with his SPLA captors. He claimed he came from "cattle people" and that he had not had a formal education: *"My cattle were my school."*

He said he was the head of the El Muhammed clan of the Rezeigat tribe. He had been recruited to the PDF in 1992 by a representative of the GOS regular army, Babikir Gasiam Asid, and was given a leadership position with responsibility for recruiting and organising PDF forces in three areas: Dhala Adabi, Safa and Sakhara. They were supplied with guns and ammunition by the GOS, but were not given any salary. He said it was GOS policy to provide the guns and encourage the PDF to fight on their behalf, keeping whatever they could capture as their reward:

> *We were armed by the GOS to fight; we were asked to collect children, sheep, goats and cattle and we used to burn some houses. Whatever was taken belonged to the PDF and was our income.*

He said that children who were captured in raids were brought up as slaves by their captors, being used to look after livestock or to do domestic work. He said that slavery was still practised because:

the president of this country doesn't say it shouldn't. But, if the president said it should not happen, it wouldn't happen. But while the president doesn't stop it, the people continue, thinking it is allowed and is normal... no one has forbidden it.

He described the significance of the train journey between El Obeid and Wau:

The train comes from the north to the south, taking troops and weapons to the south. When it returns, it returns with people.

He said that he was being well treated:

Since I was captured, no one has beaten me – even with something as small as this (holding up a very small twig from a tree). I feel very at home. I have even started learning how to mend fishing nets.

Conclusion

The stories we have recorded here of people who have suffered slavery are a sample taken from a larger collection. They are typical in that they illustrate the compelling consistency of the detailed accounts of the experience of slavery in these parts of Sudan over those years. The details recounted in individual stories are corroborated by the accounts of the community leaders, the Arab traders from the north and the mujahidin prisoner of war.

The composite picture that emerges is one of a systematic policy of enslavement as a weapon of war designed to destroy African communities and African culture. There is also the additional element of the use of slavery by the Islamist NIF "Government of Sudan" to enforce its policy of Islamisation of those who are not already Muslims, and Arabisation of the

African peoples of Bahr el-Ghazal and the Nuba Mountains (a policy which is being continued today in Darfur).

Although international pressure did begin to force the Government of Sudan to initiate mechanisms for the identification and return of some of those who have been enslaved, and although the Peace Agreement that has been signed should facilitate this process, the numbers who have been returned still fall far short of those who were abducted. Many will never return: countless numbers died in transit or during slavery; others were sold on to destinations from which they can never be rescued.

For those who do return, the problems are legion. The world as they knew it has been devastated: families have often been killed; homes, schools, clinics, crops and livestock have been destroyed, and hopes for the kind of "normal" life that they could have expected are dashed. There is a "lost generation" of children who have had no schooling; girls who have been forced into sexual relationships with their owners are likely to find it hard to marry men of their own age group – many of whom will have been killed anyway; and the destruction of the infrastructure of health and educational facilities has left a vacuum of provision of the essentials for attempts to achieve any "normalisation" of community life.

Therefore, the aftermath of this brutal policy of systematic enslavement continues to afflict the peoples of these parts of Sudan. For all, the nightmares of the anguish they had to endure as slaves will be ineradicable. For many, those nightmares are now accompanied by new and living nightmares of trying to survive in conditions of acute and multiple deprivation.

They urgently need help – but for too many, it is not forthcoming.

The world looked the other way while they were slaves and during the war in which they were enslaved. The media eventually arrived, when the catastrophe in Darfur eventually hit the headlines – but the media were too late for the

2 million dead and 5 million displaced who were victims of the NIF before Darfur.

Now the NIF is continuing its genocidal policies in Darfur, with a death toll that exceeds that of the tsunami, as it continues to kill, rape and loot and perpetrate its brutal policies with impunity.

In so far as the media have highlighted the NIF-induced tragedies of Darfur, they have diverted attention from the plight of those who are still suffering from the aftermath of the war in other parts of Sudan – and from the slavery which was a weapon of that war. This suffering continues, largely unrecorded and unrecognised.

Their cry goes up: "How long?"

NORTHERN UGANDA

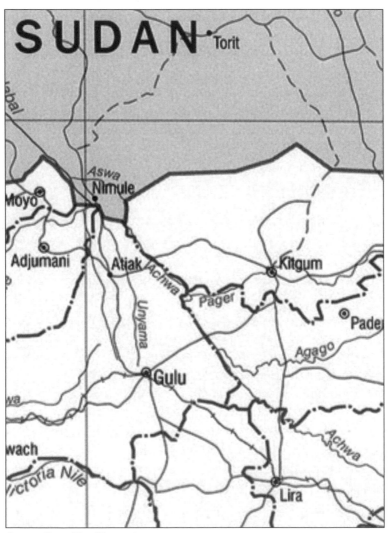

Source: Central Intelligence Agency

CHAPTER TWO

Let the Abducted Children of Uganda Speak

The Situation in Northern Uganda

While most of the Ugandan nation has enjoyed relative peace and security in recent years, the north has been wracked by civil war, caused by the relentless campaign of insurgency waged by the so-called Lord's Resistance Army (LRA). Its ruthless policies have reduced northern areas to a state of devastation: villages have been systematically attacked, property destroyed, people slaughtered and driven off their lands. Now 95% of the one and a quarter million people in the region have been herded into vast camps, which can be called "concentration camps" in respect of the dense overcrowding and lack of adequate water, sanitation, food and other amenities such as health care and education. 1,000 people a week die because of the conditions in these camps.

But the most horrifying hallmark of the LRA's insurgency is its policy of systematic abduction of children, brutalising and terrorising them and forcing them to fight as soldiers in the LRA against their own people. They are also forced to abduct other children and to maltreat them in the ways in which they themselves were maltreated.

The general situation in northern Uganda and the appalling conditions in which people try to survive amid severe overcrowding have been described by Olara A. Otunnu, the former UN Under-Secretary-General and Special

Representative For Children in Armed Conflict, in this excerpt from the Sydney Peace Prize lecture given in November 2005:

> *The human-rights and humanitarian catastrophe unfolding in northern Uganda is a methodical and comprehensive genocide, conceived and being carried out by the government. An entire society is being systematically destroyed – physically, culturally, emotionally, socially and economically – in full view of the international community. In the sobering words of Father Carlos Rodriguez, a Catholic missionary priest in the region,*
>
> > *Everything Acholi (the largest tribe affected in northern Uganda) is dying.*
>
> Or, as Médecins Sans Frontières (MSF) has reported:
>
> > *The extent of suffering is overwhelming... according to international benchmarks, this constitutes an emergency out of control.*
>
> *I know of no recent or present situation where all the elements that constitute genocide, under the Convention on the Prevention and Punishment of Genocide (1948), have been brought together in such a chillingly comprehensive manner, as in northern Uganda today.*

The Abduction, Brutalisation and Slaughter of Children

It is impossible to ascertain how many children have been abducted by the LRA, how many have perished at the hands of the LRA during "training" or how many have been killed in fighting against the Ugandan Army. The most conservative estimates give a minimum figure of 20,000 children abducted; others believe the figure may exceed 40,000.

During a visit to Gulu, Kitgum, Pader and the surrounding areas in February 2006, we met some of the children who survived abduction and were able to escape from the LRA. Their voices must speak for many others – some of whose voices will never be heard, because, as we hear, they will never live to tell of their fate.

These stories have a chilling consistency combined with a horrifying individuality, reflecting the systematic nature of LRA policies, which create and perpetuate suffering that is beyond description.

The Voices of the Children

Note: The children's full names are not given, in order to preserve anonymity. It is important for them to be able to put the past as far behind them as possible; to look ahead and not be "labelled" with their past.

(i) Daniel, 20, was abducted in 2001, tied up, beaten and deprived of water and food for three weeks. Some of those abducted died in these days. He was transferred to Juba in Sudan where, under Commander Otti, he was tortured and trained as a soldier. In April 2002, he was sent to serve under Commander Banya to attack his own village in northern Uganda, where he captured others whom he knew.

During his training, he had to undertake live shooting practice in which he had to fight fellow abductees in operations in which many died.

It was them or me.

He became increasingly *"brutal and wild"*, and escaped to find that both parents had been killed and his three brothers abducted, feared dead. He now feels strongly that all children need education.

(ii) Florence, 15, from Patongo, was abducted in 2002 and taken to Adak in Sudan. She was bound and forced to carry food, which the LRA had looted, on her head. She was kept bound for one-and-a-half weeks with virtually no food. She was given to an LRA commander as his "wife", and, as she was alone in the bush, she had to go with him. She was trained to become a soldier, given a gun and brought to Gulu. She became just like those who abducted her.

She had to fight, and on five missions she had to take other children into captivity in southern Sudan, treating them as she had been treated on the way.

> *I became wild; I didn't care about killing and I possibly became worse than them. If I had met my mother and father I would have killed them. I acted like someone who is deranged. I don't know how many people I have killed. Despite all the brainwashing, killing and becoming like the LRA, and trusting them, I wanted to escape and did so during an operation.*

She has been told that her parents are dead. Of her seven siblings, four were abducted; she is the only one to return, as the others were killed in battle.

She now lives with her grandmother, with responsibility for bringing up the surviving children. She is desperate for education but has no money to pay for it.

(iii) Daniel, 20, from Patongo, was abducted and remained in captivity for one year. When caught, he was tied up for three months, given hardly any food and beaten "all the time". Some of those captured at the same time as him died. They were taken to Juba (Sudan) where the LRA Commander Otti subjected them to "serious" training; another leader, Brigadier Banya, also trained them and they were taken to northern Uganda to fight with guns. During the training in Juba, they were taught how to parade and handle guns. Then they were given live ammunition, divided into groups and told to engage in "real" fighting against each other, so they killed each other. Those who survived were conscripted into the army.

They were not indoctrinated with any ideology – only brutality. They were young and they became "wild". On July 7, 2002 they attacked Daniel's own village, dividing into smaller units and attacking from all sides. After training, when he knew he was being sent to his own village area to fight, he realised he might be able to escape. So he took extra (civilian) clothes and in the course of the fighting managed to escape to Patongo.

When he returned, he found that both his parents had been killed by the LRA and his three brothers together with his sister had all been abducted. He believes his brothers are dead but he does not know what has happened to his sister.

His impassioned request is for education, but he does not have the money.

(iv) Charles, 19, from Lukole, five miles from Patongo, was abducted in 2003. He was attending a school about 20 miles away, as there was no adequate school any nearer. Driving there with his father, they were ambushed. He was abducted and his father was killed while trying to escape. He was taken to Juba, on foot. For three days, he was tied; then he was released in order to carry a very heavy gun (the type used for ambushing vehicles), together with another boy.

He was captured by Commander Okuti. He began military training at Juba, but when trouble developed in that area they were moved deeper into Sudan. On the way back, they were raiding and looting villages when they captured a Sudanese civilian man. He was told to kill this man – or else he himself would be killed. They were then deployed to Uganda in a 23-strong unit, where they had to fight Ugandan soldiers. Only nine of his group survived; they then had to fight another group, and many more died. He was in the bush for 18 months with the LRA. Their strategy was to make the abduction of children their priority.

> *I became wild and didn't care if I killed. I have no idea how many I killed in crossfire. The LRA taught us that we had no opportunity to return home and that, if we did so, we would find our parents dead. "There is no home for you – the only thing you can do is to fight and to overthrow the Government of Uganda." I had to pretend; I knew it wasn't true. In one confrontation, the fighting was very*

intense and hot and I was left alone with my gun. I left it to go to the river for a drink and I was taken by Ugandan soldiers. I spent two days in the barracks and was then taken to World Vision. My mother is blind and in another camp.

(v) Grace, twelve, from Oporot, was abducted in January 2005 while going to collect firewood, together with three other girls.

I don't know what has happened to the other three – they may be dead. I was taken as a child carer for one of the LRA officers, to look after his two babies, as their mother was a soldier. When one of the children was killed, I escaped. Both my parents have died of HIV. My brother has taken responsibility for us, but it is very difficult, as he is traumatised, and keeps shouting, screaming and saying that it is not his fault that his parents have died and protesting that he "never asked the soldiers to destroy their lives". It is very tough in the camp...

(vi) Bosco, 26, from Grula Lela, was abducted in 1997 and returned in 2001. He was taken from his hut while making a mat, beaten, repeatedly stamped on and hit with the butt of a gun. He had been alone in the hut. He was then forced to march to Sudan for eight months under Commander Otti. During this time, he was subjected to near-starvation, being told that this was to make him more aggressive. Training began at 3am, involving hard physical exercise, training with guns with targets in trees, and learning the local language. They were given one small meal a day at 6pm. After 18 months he began active service in Uganda with a major battle on the border, being told: *"If you have no fear, you will never be killed."* He replied: *"I have no fear."*

He never killed anyone at close quarters but did in battle. He abducted and looted, often severely beating men, women and children, but he never raped because he had been instructed: *"If you rape, you may be killed in battle."*

For four years he was involved in cross-border conflict,

during which he felt he was becoming very brutal; when alone he felt very sad. One evening, at 7pm, he escaped after being beaten up by two people on the Commander's orders because he had gone to eat after a long battle, before preparing the Commander's bed. Although he had no idea of his location, he ran through the forest, where he found a path which led to a road that led to Potang.

(vii) Joyce, 11, from Labamach Pajule. She doesn't know when she was abducted, but was taken with her mother and sister to Lapule, in the bush. She wasn't beaten, but was made to carry heavy pots on her head (the roughened skin on the scalp is still visible). After one week, her mother and sister were sent home because they were older and the LRA wanted to concentrate on young abductees. She was not involved in fighting, wasn't harmed and always remained in Uganda.

She was released because she was so weak.

(viii) Richard, 22, from Wangduku West, abducted March 5, 1999 was sleeping in his hut, alone, as his mother had died and his brothers had left. He was taken with other abductees to Welle, about 15km away, in a single file (not tied up); he was beaten and made to carry a heavy load of fresh cassava. En route, the soldiers slaughtered a large goat and hung it around his neck. He was taken to Sudan (Rubanga Tek), where he was trained under Commander Otti. He excelled at his training and was very good at firing at targets in the tree.

His first active encounter was in Sudan in the UPDF operation "Iron Fist". Then the LRA fled and he had to climb a very steep mountain where Kony, the notorious LRA leader, was stationed. Many abductees either slipped accidentally to their death or, if they faltered, the Commander shot them and they rolled to their death.

He returned to Uganda, where he was involved in much fighting and abduction in the Patongo locality. He didn't beat the abductees, but tied them up and escorted them. During this time, he claims he was forced to do three things:

- to rape a woman publicly;
- to kill another abductee with a hoe;
- and to throw an abductee down a well.

He received injuries from torture and on one occasion he was beaten repeatedly with a bicycle chain, after which he passed blood in his urine. The beating was punishment for taking too long to push the abductee down the well.

In one battle he was shot in the leg and captured by the UPDF, and was taken to the Rehabilitation Centre in 2003. While there, he learned that the LRA had killed his mother because he had escaped – she was beaten to death. His father had died before he had been abducted. He had one brother who had also been abducted but came under a different command; his brother was then transferred to his unit, whereupon he arranged his escape.

He has two sisters, one unmarried, with a child. He feels there has been a big change in his life, because he is now loved.

(ix) Irene, 15, from Latwong, was abducted in 2001. The LRA came to the village, near Pajule, and attacked for much of the night. She had fled into one of the huts where the only two occupants were wives of UPDF soldiers. She was abducted but neither tied nor beaten. She was made to carry the commander's heavy bag. During 19 months with the LRA, she was transferred to two different commanders' units. She didn't receive intensive training but during captivity she was made to kill, using three methods.

Abductees would be tied up and the neck cut with a panga knife; or the belly would be slashed open with a panga knife; or they would be beaten to death.

She was warned that if she failed to comply they would cut her neck so that she would bleed to death – and to prove it they cut her neck superficially in two places (scars just visible).

She knows she killed ten abductees (children and adults) by slashing the belly, scooping up the blood and placing it in her mouth. On another occasion, she was cooking for the commander when the UPDF came. She ran and left the food on the fire; the food burnt, and as a consequence she was beaten unconscious.

She escaped early one morning when she went to collect water for the commander's bath. She walked for one mile down the road and left the water container; she then ran through the bush and made her way towards home. She was picked up by the UPDF, and transferred to the police and then to the rehabilitation centre on June 3, 2003.

Talking about the killing, she explains how she was indoctrinated to understand that if she did not kill the abductee, then the panga knife would be given over for the abductee to kill her. She felt it was wrong.

She is now in school, but cannot concentrate and has repeated nightmares about the first killing, which occurred at dawn, and the first time she had to drink blood.

(x) Jannet, 16, now with one child, was abducted aged thirteen and remained in captivity for one year. She named her child Ronald Kinyera ("They are laughing at me"). His father is an LRA soldier. She escaped during a battle when she was four months pregnant and was walking in the bush for three months. She saw UPDF soldiers, and finally saw some people whom she recognised, from her own area. When she approached them, they were very happy to see her.

There were seven in the group in which she was abducted, three of whom had been released, and she found this very hard. When the soldiers brought her to the barracks, she was only detained for four hours, during which she was treated very well. She was taken straight to a rehabilitation centre where she gave birth, after which she returned to her home village, where she found only her mother still alive. Her two brothers had been killed by the LRA while she was in captivity; her father had died of disease before her abduction.

It is a hard time remembering things. The memories are going away but they keep coming back.

(xi) Pamela, 16, was abducted at the age of ten and held captive for six years. She now has one child, Ayee Rwot (which means "I have accepted the Lord"), aged nine months. She was taken with her older brother, whom she has never seen again. On capture all the girls were taken into a yard and divided between different men. She was given to one man, was heavily beaten and had to endure much walking, carrying heavy loads – and there was never enough food. When asked if she knew how many people she had killed, she replied: *"When you are fighting, you can never tell how many you kill."*

She spent four years in Sudan, training and fighting, and two years in Uganda. She escaped when they were patrolling through mountains; they were attacked by a helicopter gunship: the group scattered and then regrouped; they were scattered a second time; on this occasion, she escaped.

She met some government troops who were Acholi by tribe and were kind to her. One was not, but the others rebuked him. She was taken to the Agorno barracks and then to the Kitgum barracks and then to Kicwa Rehabilitation Centre for three months before going home, where she found her mother and three younger brothers; her father had died when she was young.

When asked if she still had disturbing memories, she replied: *"They are so big and so many; they are always so vivid. I see the faces."*

(xii) Alice, 16, was abducted when she was ten. She was held captive for four years, during which she gave birth to a child, Akanyo Immaculata (the first name meaning "I have borne a problem"), now one year old.

When abducted, she was in a group of about 20 schoolchildren, who were taken from the Rac Koko Camp. Some have come back; some she knew died in Sudan of diarrhoea or in the fighting. They were all badly beaten. The leader would sometimes select one of the abductees to kill and they all had to participate in the killing.

I myself helped to kill four children.

The leaders always ordered those who tried to escape to be killed.

She escaped in July 2004, when she was part of a group sent to Pader to uproot cassava from civilian fields. She and a friend quietly left the group and hid in cover by the roadside. They watched the rebels looking for them. After the rebels had passed by, they went a different way until they met a civilian. He took them to the Pader barracks, where the soldiers were kind to them and kept them there for two weeks. She said she was not assaulted and she did not have to do any work while she was there. She was then taken to a reception centre in Pader, where she spent two months before going home. Her baby was born during her stay there. Both her parents were at home; all her brothers had died very young. Her father and mother were both very happy to see her and they both love her – as do the majority of people in her village.

> *But some are not happy with me. They think my child, born of the LRA, has an evil spirit."*
>
> *Even up until today, the memories come back, especially when I wake up from my sleep; they go down but then they rise up again. I see those I killed.*

(xiii) Betty, 18, was abducted when she was ten and held captive for eight years. She has two children – the first born during captivity. The older child, Ajok Immaculata, is now four; the younger is Rubanga Ngeyo – a boy aged six months (his name means "God knows", which she said means that God knows how much she has suffered).

When she was abducted, she was taken with two other children. They both escaped before her and she has since seen them both. Betty was often beaten when first taken prisoner and the beatings continued throughout the eight years; she also suffered from constant hunger from the meagre food allowance.

She was not involved in any fighting but she was made to do the cooking and to look after children. However, early in her captivity, she was twice ordered to kill two recently abducted children, helping others to club them to death with heavy branches.

She escaped when she was sent in a group to steal food – not during a battle. She and four others put the food down and left together. They slept overnight in the bush and then found a civilian, who took them to the police, who then took them to the army barracks in Pader. She spent four days there, and then she was taken to the Rakelo Centre in Lira, where she spent one month before going home, where she found her father and one younger brother. Her father was very happy to see her.

> *But other people don't look on me well; they say that I and my baby have brought evil spirits on us and my children are not allowed to play with other children. Most feel this.*

(xiv) Christine, 17, was abducted when she was ten and held captive for six years. She now has two children. The elder, Adeno Can, is a boy aged five whose name means "I have suffered severely"; the younger is Rwot Ogonya, a one-year-old girl whose name means "The Lord released me".

When asked whether she had ever had to kill, Christine replied:

> *If you don't kill, you will yourself be killed. We killed many children; I don't know how many – but many, many.*

But she said she was always praying to God, asking him to set her free.

When she returned home she found that one of her brothers had been killed by the LRA, her home had been burnt down and her parents had died in the blaze. Her younger brother had been staying with their uncle at the time of the attack and they now live together in the camp.

> *Memories come back, especially when I sleep, of those I killed. The exact picture of them.*

Their uncle does not now help them much:

I am not happy as there is no one to stand up for me.

(xv) James (very traumatised and withdrawn), age unknown (he looked about eight to ten), has just escaped, having spent three years in the bush. He was abducted from the fields while helping his parents and was taken to the border to work for a commander. One day he was sent as a scout to an area that he knew, so he took the opportunity to escape. He said that, as he was so young (pointing to a little girl walking by, aged about five), they couldn't abuse him too much.

(xvi) Sunday, 18, was abducted in 2001. This was the time when her family were moving to the camp and they were returning to fetch their belongings. She was abducted at a nearby village, where she found a large number of children who had also been abducted. They were tied up and given ideological training, being told that they were to overthrow the Ugandan government. They were taken to Juba and beyond. They were given 50 lashes and fed with looted food, and began training.

> *If you behaved well, you were treated better. When someone tried to escape, everyone was lined up and forced to beat the escapee to death. They taught us where to hit. I did this three times.*
>
> *We were given military training, in handling guns, and fitness training for three months. Then we were given guns and told to loot food from villages in Uganda. We attacked people when they were going to fetch water and we killed them if they resisted. We inflicted on others the kind of initiation that had been inflicted on us, so we handed it on to others.*

She recalled an incident in which they were ambushed by Government soldiers; two LRA soldiers were killed; they then overpowered three Ugandan soldiers, whom they killed. There was another occasion when some people whom she knew were abducted; she reported this and was taken away while they killed the abductees. She escaped in November 2003.

(xvii) Nekanore, 18, from Pajule. In 2003, he was going by bike to get food when he was ambushed. Two boys had already been captured and he was put with them. Two soldiers were guarding them. They were tied together with rope around their waists and given loads to carry to Teso. A helicopter gunship bombed them "en route". They were now a group of about 60, of whom 20 died and ten were seriously injured. If they were abductees, they were left to die. They were there for a week, during which time they were bombed every day. A radio message from Joseph Kony ordered them to go to Katiri in Sudan to reach him within six days. They found that there was a strategy meeting of commanders, including Arabs as well as LRA.

Then an order was issued for 400 to return to fight in Uganda.

As they crossed the border, they were attacked by a helicopter gunship, which killed 80 of the 400, many dying instantly, others from severe injuries. LRA Commander Agweng was injured and he was carried away. The fighting was so intense because it was open territory. They were subjected to constant bombardment, living with only water, hardly any food and no medicine for the wounded. They tried to get oil from trees to help the injured.

The group was now reduced and divided into a smaller unit of 60, which was ordered to the other side of Gulu; the rest remained where they were. They walked for two days without food, and were attacked again and again. Eventually only six were left together, living on wild honey for four days. Then the remnant reunited, but eight more died in another ambush. Many other abductees encountered Government soldiers and suffered helicopter attacks during which very many more died.

He was in the bush for one year. The number of children available for abduction was diminishing, as they were now taking shelter in the towns, so they attacked adults fetching water and firewood. They took about 18–20 to a collection point to be taken to Sudan.

The LRA instructed them to concentrate on abducting children because they can forget their past. Adults were mainly used for forced labour as porters.

He felt that, in the same way as they had been abducted, they would treat others similarly.

He spent three months in the same area as Kony and saw how many Arabs visited him. Kony would not allow them to take any of the abducted children, as he wanted the children to fight in Uganda.

Kony was brutal. For example, when he was addressing a large crowd, if he saw women he didn't like, he called them witches and had them killed.

Nekanore escaped during an ambush in which the unit was scattered. He and another abductee walked to Azero, where they surrendered to Ugandan soldiers in March 2004.

(xviii) Monica, 18, from Lukole in Pader, was abducted in 2003 from her home at night. Her brother had already been abducted – she eventually met him a year later in Sudan, before they were separated again.

She was tied up, beaten and shot in the leg (scars still clearly visible) during an ambush. She was not given any treatment.

She was taken to Sudan for military training and was "given" to Commander Palaro. She became pregnant and gave birth with no help at all.

I was just treated like an animal.

She had to go to fight in Uganda, carrying her baby with her. She fought in Teso and Lango and was ordered to carry out abductions, especially of children. If any resisted, they were immediately killed.

She has had to kill time and again: *"In a battle, one has to kill."*

During one confrontation not far from her village, she met a woman whom she knew and asked her to take her child, now 18 months old, because she could not continue to carry her gun and the child at the same time. She left her daughter, Apio Consulate, in the area of Lacek Ocot and she has not seen her again.

When she escaped, she walked a long way and sat by the road alone without any water. She asked a gentleman who was walking by for some water and he brought her to safety last month.

Monica's father was killed by a helicopter gunship. She desperately wants to go to school, as she was studying at secondary school when she was abducted.

(xix) Alice, 16 years old, from Korolalogi village, was abducted in 2002. This was early one morning while it was still dark and she was asleep at home. She was sharing a room with six other girls. Her parents were not around. Members of the LRA woke them all up and captured six of them. One girl escaped and was not abducted. The girls were given sacks of beans, maize and sorghum to carry. This was loot stolen from the village. They were forced to walk with other villagers (hundreds of other villagers had been abducted with them) around ten to twelve miles with their loads. One girl became tired and was unable to carry her sack further. The LRA killed her by striking her head with a heavy axe. Her body was left where it fell. When night came, they were allowed to sleep.

On the next morning, the girls were forced to parade in front of the LRA soldiers with no tops (blouses, shirts) on. They were then beaten. In reply to a question asking why she believed the LRA did this, Alice answered that the LRA members were making them scared so that they would not escape. UPDF (Uganda Government) helicopters then flew overhead, bombing the site. Many of the group (abductees and LRA soldiers) were killed and the others scattered throughout the countryside. She and three of the other girls with whom she had been sharing a room tried to escape but were recaptured.

They were then forced to walk to Sudan. One of the girls, Alice's sister, died of cholera on the way.

When they arrived in Sudan, the remaining girls were distributed to become wives of LRA soldiers. Alice's "husband's" first name was Oyo. She cannot reveal his surname. She was mistreated and beaten often. The man had many other wives too. When asked why she was beaten, Alice said that this was to force her to have sex with the man because she did not love him. She lived in the bush in this manner for two years. When asked what kind of brainwashing she received or what words the LRA soldiers repeated often, she said that she was warned not to escape because the LRA would soon overthrow the Government. Alice was never told why she was abducted.

She was able to escape one night, with another girl who had to leave two children behind. She walked for two weeks and reached Gulu in January 2006. UPDF soldiers fired on them, however, and the two girls were separated. While in captivity, she saw many people die and be killed and now she suffers from nightmares. She has not yet gone back home to her family. Her father was killed by the LRA but she has heard that six of her brothers and sisters are at her home with their mother.

(xx) Josephine, 18 years old, from Gulela village, was abducted and taken to Sudan in 2004. She was in the fourth year of primary school. She was visiting her uncle's house when the LRA soldiers came. UPDF soldiers were also in the area. Josephine had woken up at around 4am to go to the toilet. She saw men with guns around but she assumed these were Government UPDF soldiers. She went back into her house. An hour or so later, she heard gunfire. The LRA and UPDF soldiers exchanged bullets. She did not know where to run and ended up running into LRA soldiers. They abducted her and many other people from the village. She was forced to carry two crates of soda. Others had to carry salt, sugar and other loot. They walked two miles very slowly because they had to keep hidden from Government soldiers. Some of the abductees had to carry wounded LRA soldiers. Those who became tired because of the heavy load were killed; about half of the abductees lost their lives in this manner. LRA soldiers would ask people if they wanted to rest. If they said yes, they were killed. An LRA soldier slashed their heads off. The body would be left where it fell. The survivors eventually reached Sudan.

The first LRA soldier who had abducted Josephine made her his wife. He had no other wives. She was beaten to force her to have sex with him. She did not have any children. She stayed in the bush with the LRA for about one and a half years. Her "husband" would leave her in the care of other abductees (young boys) when he went away for ambushes and attacks in Gulu. The young boys were from her area so they were good to her.

When asked if she was brainwashed or what phrases were repeated by the LRA soldiers, she said that she was told that, if she returned to her home, the Government soldiers would rape her repeatedly, using a full basin of condoms, until she died; so it was better for her to remain with the LRA.

Abductees who had been with the LRA for some time were allowed to listen to the radio. She was able to listen to Radio Omega from Gulu. She heard that abductees who returned were treated well. She then felt encouraged to plan to escape. Many of the other abductees were too brainwashed by the LRA to think of escaping even after hearing the radio reports.

On the day that she escaped, the whole group was going to set up ambushes on roads around Gulu. She was assigned to a group led by Otti, second in command to Kony. Her job was to find loot and carry it back to the bush. They ambushed a car on a road near Gulu. As they were carrying the loot back, some of the group branched off to find fruit. She asked if she could go and pee. She was given permission, and ran off into the bush. Some of the LRA realised she had gone and followed her. They could not find her. She hid in a forest and, when she was sure that they had given up, she walked on to Gulu. She returned in October 2005.

Josephine arrived at a school in Gulu and was arrested by UPDF soldiers. They kept her for an hour or so before they took her to a Caritas centre. The UPDF soldiers were brusque and shouted accusations at her. They did not beat her, though. They kept asking her if she knew what the LRA's plans were. She did not know. Eventually they released her.

She had five brothers and sisters. Her father was killed by the LRA when she was very young. One of her brothers had been killed by the rebels in 2004. He had been abducted. He got tired when carrying loot and was killed.

Since her return in October 2005, Josephine has had trouble sleeping. She said that everyone in the rehabilitation centre has nightmares. She has at times screamed the place down, shouting that someone is being killed. It is only in the last two weeks (since the beginning of February 2006) that she has been able to sleep. She said that counselling is provided for recently returned abductees but after one or two months they receive no more counselling. She has been offered training in a tailoring school.

Conclusion

The stories recounted by these young people, who were mere children when abducted by the LRA, reveal an appalling consistency in their detailed and horrifying accounts of the systematic policies of intimidation, brutalisation and terror to which they were subjected.

These are the relatively "lucky" ones, who have managed to escape and return to their own people. Never heard will be the voices of the children killed while in the hands of the LRA: such as those shot by these very children to whom we were speaking when they were forced to take part in military exercises against each other, using live ammunition; or the abductee pushed down a well by one of our interviewees, who was forced to carry out this act (and subsequently beaten with a bicycle chain because he took "too long" to accomplish it); or the countless children killed in military action against the Ugandan Army.

But, even for these "lucky" ones, life is very harsh and they face many difficulties. Many testify to the recurring memories and nightmares of their hellish experiences with the LRA. For many others, their escape was marred by the discovery that family members had been abducted or killed by the LRA, or had died of disease (especially HIV/AIDS). Some found that their local communities were less than welcoming, especially of their babies, conceived as a result of enforced sexual relationships with LRA soldiers. Many girls will find it hard or impossible to find "good" husbands, given their previous sexual experiences.

And all have returned to a situation in northern Uganda that is desperate. With 95% of the population forced off their lands to live in overcrowded camps, without adequate water, sanitation or health care, crowded into cramped tukuls, the quality of life for those who are forced to live there is abysmal.

Many of the children and young people who suffered as abductees are now desperate for education. But, even if a secondary school is available, often they cannot pay the fees and cannot obtain the education they need to escape from despair and the poverty trap.

As with the slaves of Sudan, freedom does not bring an end to suffering. The nightmares of the past remain and are accompanied by new forms of suffering, destitution and vulnerability.

There are organisations providing help. But the needs and numbers far outweigh their capacity. They need support to reach more of the young people who have suffered so much. In the meantime, the fate of some of those who have escaped may be a case of running from the frying pan into the fire – as illustrated by the following article, *"From Captivity to Slavery"*.

Appendix

FROM CAPTIVITY TO SLAVERY
Frank Nyakairu
Monitor Publications

It was started as a farm to help formerly abducted children from the LRA war make a living. Labora farm has, however, turned out to be a place where, under the same structure as the LRA, the abductees are tortured.

Even when in pain from a wound to his left eye socket, the result of a gunshot, 15-year-old Denis Okonya was never allowed to seek treatment. Okonya was shot in a gun battle in June 2003, with a bullet ripping across his face, and is now one-eyed. Instead, his bosses, who also just happen to be his former captors, accused him of trying to dodge work.

No longer in rebel Lord's Resistance Army (LRA) captivity, Okonya and scores of formerly abducted children find themselves still working under some of their former rebel commanders – this time on the government-founded Labora Farm in Gulu. With little or no government or civil-society monitoring, a *Daily Monitor* investigation found that abuses such as forced labour are common on the 50-acre farm that grows food crops such as maize and soybeans for sale.

Captured in action in 2004, Brig. Kenneth Banya, said to have once been the LRA's number three, is the master of Labora Farm, located 14km outside Gulu in Koro sub-county. Lt Col. Francis Okwang, who deputised for him in the bush, maintains the same position at Labora, alongside other assistants.

The LRA stands accused of carrying out mass killings, abduction, maiming and killing an estimated 20,000 children, according to the United Nations. In captivity, the children are turned into sex slaves and child soldiers.

The 20-year war has also displaced about 1.5 million people who are crowded into squalid camps in parts of Acholi, Lango and Teso sub-regions.

When the International Criminal Court first took interest in the workings of the LRA in November 2003, Banya was on the wanted list but he was taken off when he entered a "deal" with the Government. Today he lives at the UPDF senior quarters in Gulu and is lined up to testify on behalf of the Government in its treason case against Forum for Democratic Change leader Kizza Besigye. The Government claims that Besigye attempted to make common cause with the LRA, a charge he has strongly denied. The LRA is designated locally and internationally as a terrorist group.

Labora Farm

When the Government drew up the Shs 54m Labora Farm proposal a few years ago, donors shied away for unclear reasons. But, under the Northern Uganda Social Action Fund, the Ugandan government funded the programme. And so the farm came into being late in 2004 to help homeless returnees make a living. Well, it has turned out to be, as one humanitarian worker described it:

> *a transit labour camp where traumatised ex-LRA abductees are tormented and abused under the same structure as that of the LRA.*

It is a description echoed by a number of ex-LRA returnees working on the farm:

> *I could not be allowed to go for treatment even when I once told the commander that my eye was hurting. He shouted at me and told me that I'm giving excuses to dodge work*

The boy, who was abducted in 2000, lost his left eye in June 2003 to bomb shrapnel during the Teso invasion. He escaped in November 2005 and started working at Labora Farm in the hope of getting money to treat his eye.

I have worked there for months now [but] I have been given nothing. I have decided to leave and try something else,

the one-eyed Okonya said.

Okonya, who is still stuck at the farm because he lost both parents in the war, is not the only complainant. Two young women, Ms Joyce Ayot and Ms Lucy Achat, also claim they were harassed and humiliated by the male commanders.

Recently, after working, I tried to get onto the truck to come back to town, but Okwang Alero pushed me off and told me to walk 14km in the night back home,

Achat said.

Another time, when I tried to take some food home, he slashed my polythene bag open and my maize poured in the garden.

Lt Col. Alero is one of Banya's lieutenants at Labora:

Alero... hurls very obscene insults at us and threatens violence all the time,

Achat complained further.

Both women said Banya is "a good man" who must address Alero's behaviour.

Having worked on the farm for more than a year without pay from the proceeds as earlier promised, Ayot and Achat abandoned Labora for casual labour in Gulu town.

The farm is composed of seven gardens, each headed by an ex-LRA officer. One such officer is Major Jackson Acama, who escaped in 2004 after 17 years with the LRA. The army and local authorities in Gulu have been criticised for letting him stay with the four wives he returned with from the bush. The wives, including two teenage mothers, also work at Labora. *"They want to be with me,"* he told the *Daily Monitor.* *"Even when one was stolen by her family she escaped back to me."*

A probe of the farm carried out in May 2005 by Gulu Save the Children Organisation (Gusco), but not made public, indicates that the ex-rebel commanders were threatening such teenage mothers if they abandoned their husbands from the bush.

> *Some girls were a bit concerned at the utterances made by the leaders about their sexual lives with other people who were once not abducted and that all of them must get formerly abducted partners. That Labora is one way they will use to put an end to such relationships,*

the report says.

It also talks of:

> *beatings and forceful hard labour without food for both the mother and the child.*
>
> *There is totally nothing wrong with Labora Farm; if there is anything else, I will talk to you later,*

Banya said on the phone, having repeatedly declined a meeting because he was reportedly busy.

Accountability needed

The outgoing LC-V Chairman of Gulu, Lt Col. Walter Ochora, under whose tenure the project was established, has suggested that the ex-commanders be audited and withdrawn owing to what he described as "psychological euphoria". *"I have read very terrible things in a Unicef report about the project,"* he said.

> *It was well intended but now I do not see its future. If NGOs are arguing that these kids [who were] enslaved in the bush still feel the same, let the commanders be withdrawn.*

But before they are withdrawn, as Ochora rightly notes, questions about accountability have to be answered.

Maize, beans, soybeans and potatoes are some of the food crops grown on the 50 acres of farmland. According to the ex-abductees, more than 80% of the produce is sold off in food markets. Each harvest season, every one of the seven gardens produces crops worth about Shs 2m. With two harvest seasons in a year, sources have valued annual income from Labora at approximately Shs 20m, but none of the returnees who worked at Labora has benefited.

"Sometimes, they do not even give us any food after harvesting," said one of the workers.

When the Uganda Human Rights Commission took interest, the Regional Rights Officer, Mr Francis Ogwang, said: *"Banya told me that they had plunged the money back into the farm and the first beneficiary would receive this year."*

Ochora said he did not know how much had been made from the farm and suggested an audit. With this controversy, the Gusco report recommended that Labora be closed or handed to different people to manage.

It is one of many reports on Labora submitted to the United Nations agencies and the Uganda Human Rights Commission, but little or nothing at all has been done.

A report on the UN website describes goings-on at Labora as "problematic practices".

BURMA

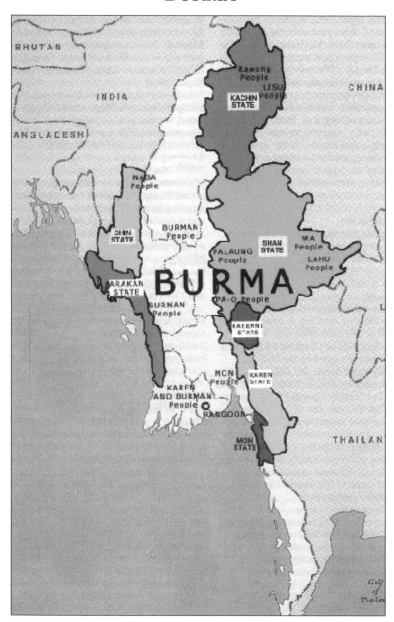

Source: *A Land Without Evil* by Benedict Rogers, Monarch Books, 2004

CHAPTER THREE

Let the Sex Slaves, Forced Porters and Child Soldiers of Burma Speak

Introduction

Burma, renamed Myanmar in 1989 by the present military regime, is the largest country in mainland South East Asia. This beautiful land has become a place of hell for many of its citizens. They are currently ruled by one of the world's most oppressive regimes, with the Orwellian name of "The State Peace and Development Council" (SPDC). This is the latest in a succession of military regimes that have ruled Burma since Ne Win seized power in a coup in 1962.

Elections were held in 1990 and were won convincingly by the National League for Democracy (NLD), led by Nobel Laureate Daw Aung San Suu Kyi. But the military regime rejected the results, imprisoned many of the victorious democratically elected politicians, and intensified its grip on power. Daw Aung San Suu Kyi has now been under house arrest for over ten years.

The regime systematically oppresses all who oppose it and has been pursuing ruthless policies of attempted cultural genocide against the many ethnic national groups who make up 35% of Burma's diverse population. These include the Karen, Karenni and Shan peoples in eastern Burma, the Chin, Kachin and Rohingya peoples to the west and the Mon in the south.

In areas that are occupied by SPDC troops, policies of oppression and persecution include the systematic use of forced labour on a massive scale and the use of some of those who have been forced to be porters as human minesweepers. The conditions in which the porters have to work are so harsh that many perish: elderly people and pregnant women may have to carry loads of 30kg (60lbs) of rice or ammunition from dawn until dusk, with virtually no rest, food or water. If they fall by the wayside, they are beaten, sometimes to death. The frequency and duration of coercion to undertake forced labour often means that people cannot survive because they have no time to tend their own crops.

In parts of Burma, such as Chin State where 95% of the population is Christian, the people have been forced to destroy churches and crosses; sometimes they have been forced to help to build Buddhist pagodas in their place. Throughout Burma there are policies of discrimination against ethnic nationals, including preventing them from achieving significant promotion in any government-controlled organisation.

Worse still is the plight of ethnic national groups who resist the invasion of SPDC troops into their land. The Karen, Karenni and Shan peoples are subjected to constant military offensives as the SPDC tries to achieve military domination: their villages are attacked and burnt, then mined, so that the displaced people cannot return for their belongings or to obtain food. If captured, the civilians often face a fate worse than death, with torture, use as human minesweepers or execution. Others suffer from brutal SPDC policies of sexual exploitation. Well-documented reports give chilling evidence of the systematic use of rape as a weapon of war: "Catwalk to the Barracks" documents the horrors to which many Mon women have been subjected and "Shattering Silences" is a similarly appalling account of the fate of many Karen women (see later for examples).

Those who flee into the jungle are doomed to live in danger and deprivation – in hiding, scavenging for food, with no adequate shelter or medical care. Often they are afraid to light fires for fear of detection by SPDC soldiers, and they have no adequate means of maintaining a normal life such as growing crops or having access to education. Hundreds of thousands of such Internally Displaced People (IDPs) are currently living and dying in these harsh conditions.

At the time of writing this chapter (April 2006), our e-mail has just received this message, typical of several such messages each week, sent by the highly respected and responsible organisation "Free Burma Rangers", who support cross-border medical teams taking aid to the IDPs and obtaining information on their predicament:

> *April 6, 2006: In recent weeks over 5,000 people have been displaced in Toungoo and Nyaunglebin Districts in Karen State. Ongoing attacks by the Burma Army have intensified and there are now over 2,000 people in hiding in Toungoo District alone. People are fleeing in advance of the army, in attempts to reach the Salem River. Clusters of tens and hundreds of internally displaced people (IDPs) trek over mountains, across army-controlled roads and through mine-infested tracts of land to find their way to refugee camps. Cut off from their livelihood, the IDPs are critically short of food, medicine, shelter and support to continue their children's education while on the run (FBR).* (See photo section)

Hundreds of thousands more have fled into Thailand, where they form a vast population confined to a string of camps along the border. Although they are safe there, they are confined to these overcrowded camps, unable to leave for freedom in Thailand and only able to return to Burma at risk of their lives. They are thus trapped, unable to live normal lives, as they have no land for crops or livestock. With virtually no post-school educational facilities or career opportunities for young people, these camps are massive conurbations of people doomed to "trajectories of despair".

Burma also has the notoriety of retaining the largest number of child soldiers in the world today. 70,000 boys –

from the age of eleven upwards – have been kidnapped and forcibly recruited into the SPDC Army. Their parents are not informed of their whereabouts – they just disappear into oblivion in military training camps and then many are dispatched to the front line where their fate is unknown. A few escape – we refer to two of these later in the chapter.

All these concerns have been well documented and widely recognised. For example, many are summarised in this extract from a Resolution passed by the United Nations Commission on Human Rights on April 8, 2004:

> *Situation of Human Rights in Myanmar*
>
> *"The Commission on Human Rights*
> *expresses its grave concern:*
> *...(D) Extrajudicial killings, rape and other forms of sexual violence persistently carried out by members of the armed forces; continuing use of torture; renewed instances of political arrests and continuing detentions, including of prisoners whose sentences have expired; and prisoners held incommunicado while awaiting trial; forced relocation; destruction of livelihoods and confiscations of land by the armed forces; forced labour, including child labour; trafficking in persons; denial of freedom of assembly, association, expression and movement; discrimination and persecution on the basis of religious or ethnic background; wide disrespect for the rule of law and lack of independence of the judiciary; unsatisfactory conditions of detention; systematic use of child soldiers; and violations of the rights to an adequate standard of living, such as food, medical care and education.*

Sexual Slavery

In discussing this subject, it needs to be noted that women from these ethnic groups are highly sensitive to the stigma attached to rape. While such sensitivity is universal, the cultural norms for these societies make it perhaps particularly hard for girls and women to admit to such experiences and even more difficult to discuss them. Therefore any statistics are likely to be underestimates, as many cases are probably never even reported. However, some have given evidence of their ordeals and their testimonies have been recorded in a number of reports.

These reports have been published by reputable organisations and have documented widespread use of sexual slavery and exploitation by the SPDC. The evidence from all the different sources is corroborative and shows consistent policies of brutality and of the use of rape as a weapon of war.

Sexual Slavery of Mon Women

"Catwalk to the Barracks: Conscription of women for sexual slavery and other practices of sexual violence by troops of the Burmese military regime in Mon areas", Women and Child Rights Project (Southern Burma) and Human Rights Foundation of Monland (Burma), July 2005.[1]

This report documents systematic policies of sexual enslavement of women of the Mon people. Although there has been a ceasefire between the main Mon political party, the New Mon State Party, and the Burmese military regime, the SPDC, since 1995, Burmese Army troops are still practising systematic sexual violence.

The report details 37 incidents of sexual violence against 50 women and girls, aged fourteen to 50 years old, and reveals evidence of widespread conscription of women into sexual slavery. It also corroborates the findings of earlier reports on sexual violence in Shan and Karen States (*Licence to Rape* and *Shattering Silences* – see below for details).[2, 3] They all show the use of rape as a strategy of control and intimidation by the SPDC's troops.

> *The lack of rule of law and climate of impunity for military rape have caused SPDC's troops to become increasingly emboldened in their acts of sexual violence. Many rapes took place during military operations against armed groups still active in southern Burma, such as the Karen National Union and a Mon splinter group; SPDC troops gang-raped, beat, kicked, slashed and killed women as "punishment" for supporting rebel groups. However, sexual violence is not only occurring in areas of conflict, but in "peaceful" areas under full SPDC control. The SPDC has deployed 20 more battalions in the southern Mon area since 1998; these troops have seized land from local villagers and forced them to work on military plantations and guard infrastructure projects such as gas pipelines. The increased troop presence has caused increased incidents of rape of local women.*

The report describes how, in 2003–4, in southern Ye township:

> *SPDC troops brazenly conscripted scores of "comfort women" from nearby villages, who were forced to work for the troops by day and were forced into sexual slavery at night. They also forced about 30 young women, including schoolgirls, to stay at their base and take part in a military "fashion and beauty show".*
>
> *Over half of the documented cases of rape were committed by military officers, often in front of, or together with their troops. Many of the rapes took place in the women's homes or in other villagers' houses, frequently in the presence of other family members.*

To add insult to injury, no action has been taken against those who carried out these crimes and local community leaders who have tried to bring formal complaints have been beaten or threatened with execution. Consequently, many cases are not even reported.

Interviews with women who suffered sexual violence, including some who were subjected to the "catwalk" for the SPDC "Beauty and Fashion Shows"

(i) Name: Mi H-- L--; 19 years old; from Yain-dein village, Ye township, Mon State:

> I'm H-- L--- from Yin Dein village of southern Ye township, Mon State. In order to join in the "Fashion and Beauty Show" in Khaw-za village in the evening of Independence Day, which was managed by the local Burmese battalion, our village headman selected four young Mon ladies who were tall and slim from our village to participate in the Show.
>
> According to the order of the commander of the Burmese Army battalion, the selected girls were asked to stay in the battalion for three days and two nights. During these days, the ladies were asked to rehearse a "catwalk" in front of them (the commander and soldiers in the battalion base) and later the commander released two of the four selected girls because of their ages. These two girls were between 8th and 10th standard in their high school classes and even though they were pretty, their physical appearance was still young.
>
> The young women were also forced to do work in the army bases, such as cooking, carrying water and finding food for them during these rehearsal days. At nighttime, they were forced to entertain the battalion officers such as by massaging them, especially the commander of the battalion. But nobody knows who were raped by the soldiers and officers of the local Burmese Army battalion in the fashion and beauty show.

(ii) Mi E-- W--: 19 years old, from Khaw-za village, Ye township, Mon State:

> *My name is Mi E-- W--- from Khaw-za village (southern part of Ye township). As the local Burmese Army commander saw that I was tall and slim, he ordered our village headmen to include me in the "Fashion and Beauty Show". The commander ordered all unmarried women, who were over 5 feet and 6 inches tall to be involved in the fashion show.*
>
> *I did not want to be involved in the fashion show and so I fled from my village. Another two girls from my village were selected to be involved in the fashion show against their will. As the Burmese Army commander requested four girls to be involved in the fashion contest, the village headmen had to find two girls from town (Ye town) to be involved in the fashion show. The villagers had to pay for these hired women.*
>
> *It was not only women from our village, but they also asked ten other villages to send one to four girls to the fashion show to be involved in the contest. They also told the village headmen to select even schoolgirls, but they had to be in Grades 8 to 10. I heard they selected four girls from Yin-dein village.*
>
> *If the selected girls were not beautiful and too young (if they looked like children), they rejected them and forced the village headmen to select again.*
>
> *Those selected girls had to go to the army base (near Khaw-za village) and stay in the base for two days and two nights for rehearsal before the fashion show actually took place.*
>
> *During these days and nights, we didn't know how the commanders and soldiers treated those girls.*
>
> *According to the selected girls, they had to do a "catwalk" in front of the army commanders for hours. If the commanders were not satisfied, they were forced to keep*

walking. The commanders also came and touched their bodies and pulled at their clothes during the rehearsal.

There were about 30 girls in the whole area who were forced to be in army bases for several days for the rehearsal of the "catwalk" for the fashion show. Then, (in the second week of December 2003), the commanders held a "fashion show" contest in Khaw-za village. Girls were asked to do the "catwalk" and posed in different styles on the stage and the commanders selected the most beautiful girls and gave them small prizes.

Besides this fashion show, the young women in many villages have been constantly forced to do work in the army bases and to entertain the commanders of the Burmese Army. They asked at least three women from one village to stay at their bases for 24 hours. Those women had to do cooking, carry water and find food for them.

At night-time, the commanders forced the women to sing "karaoke" songs together with them to entertain them. The women had to serve liquor and food for them. They also had to massage them. Many women were raped, but I don't know the details.

(iii) Mi H--, 19 years old, from eastern part of Ye township:
On August 27, 1997, a column of Burmese Army troops from LIB (Light Infantry Brigade) No. 273 led by Major Lin Maung came into a Mon village, in the eastern part of Ye township. Commander Major Lin Maung of SPDC LIB 273 raped a girl, Mi H--- (19 years old), to punish her father, who was accused of contacting the KNLA's local battalion.

Soon after the troops arrived in the village, they arrested the victim's father, Nai P-- (53 years old) and tied him up in the outer open room of his house. During the interrogation, the soldiers beat him and asked him how often he had gone to meet the KNLA soldiers. The soldiers also gathered other village leaders in front of Nai P--'s house during the interrogation. While the soldiers were torturing the man, the commander, Major Lin Maung, went into the inner room of the house and pointed a gun at his daughter to rape her. The girl resisted and asked for help from her father, but the commander carried on and raped her. Although the father heard the suffering of his daughter, he could not help because of the gun pointed at him.

Other village headmen also heard the cries of the girl, but they could not help. After the rape, the commander came out from the inner room and said to the man that if he continued contacting KNLA (Karenni National Liberation Army) soldiers, he would again be punished and his daughter would be raped.

(iv) A 25-year-old housewife from Maw-khani village, Yebyu township, Tenasserim Division:
In June 1999, when Infantry Brigade No. 25 troops entered Maw-khani village, all the men in the village except the elderly fled to escape being taken as porters. Some soldiers also climbed into many villagers' houses and looted belongings and attempted to rape women.

When a low ranking officer, Corporal Myo Myint, SPDC IB (Infantry Brigade) No. 25, tried to rape Mi Myaing (25 years old), she refused and fought against him. He lost his temper and killed her by stabbing her with his army knife. She died on the spot.

This incident of attempted rape and murder was well known to the commander of IB No. 25, but no action was taken against Corporal Myo Myint.

(v) Naw B-- B-- and Naw M-- K--, 16- and 17-year-old housewives, from Kya-inn-seikyi township, Karen State:
On October 3, 1999, SPDC troops from Light Infantry Brigade No. 120 led by Lt Col. Maung Maung Oo went into this village and stayed there for one week to check who were the supporters of KNLA soldiers and wives of rebel soldiers. The Burmese soldiers arrested twelve villagers including two women. The soldiers tortured ten men by cutting the ears off some of them, as well as beating them, kicking them and burning them with

fire. The soldiers also tortured two women, Naw B-- B-- (16 years old) and Naw M-- K-- (17 years old). These two young women were married and their husbands had fled from the village to avoid being arrested by Burmese soldiers. Thus, the soldier said their husbands were Karen soldiers. They tortured the two women cruelly. First, after beating the women during interrogation, the soldiers raped them repeatedly. As the women denied that their husbands were rebel soldiers, the soldiers also cut Naw B-- B--'s breasts with a knife. Because of this serious injury, she lost consciousness. Then the soldiers also poured hot water into Naw M-- K--'s nose. Her whole face was burnt with hot water and her skin was severely damaged. Her face became totally red and severely painful. Naw M-- K-- had a four-month-old baby, and, although she asked to feed milk to her baby, the soldiers did not allow her. Her hungry baby cried for the whole day.

This rape and accompanying torture by the Burmese Army were apparently intended to instil fear into Karen villagers so that they would not contact Karen National Liberation Army (KNLA) troops.

(vi) Four married women farmers (names not given), aged between 23 and 60, from Yebyu township, Tenasserim Division:
In April 2000, when Light Infantry Brigade 104 led by Lt Col. Yatkha went into their village, the soldiers tried to arrest all the men to make them porters. This village is a Mon village with over 500 households. However, the men, who had received advance information about the arrest, fled outside the village and hid in forests and in their plantations. Therefore the soldiers were quite angry and seized some women instead from their houses to be porters.

The soldiers seized thirteen ethnic Mon women in the village: the age range of these women was between 23 and 60 years old, some married and some unmarried. The soldiers took these women for porter service in their military patrol for three days and three nights. During this service, the soldiers forced the women porters to carry about 25 kilograms of ammunition or food supplies and made them walk for the whole day with that weight. When the women could not walk as fast as the soldiers, they shouted at, beat and kicked the women porters, treating them like the male porters who had been seized from another village. During porter service, two women who could not manage to keep up with the soldiers were kicked by a sergeant.

After sunset, the soldiers grouped them in one place and let them sleep. After midnight, some soldiers came and pointed their guns at some young women and separated them from the group, and some commanders raped them. About four women (the witness did not identify their names) were separated from the group on three nights and were repeatedly raped.

(vii) Mi K-- L--, an unmarried 20-year-old woman from Yebyu township, Tenasserim Division:
During the evening of July 28, 2001, the deputy-commander of the Yapu militia force, U Aung Win, and one of his followers went and visited their friends in a village, about ten miles away from their own. While they were with their friends they drank a lot of local alcohol and by midnight had become drunk, so their friends kept their guns and said they would give them back in the morning.

The two militiamen left their friends' house and tried to climb into other villagers' houses where there were only women because their husbands were away on farms or working on fruit plantations. When they climbed into these houses, they took their knives along with them.

U Aung Win's follower climbed into the house of a woman called Ma M--. He tried to rape her by pointing his sharp knife at her. When the woman refused, he cut her hands with the knife and pointed his knife at her throat and other body parts, and then raped her. She dared not cry for help for fear of being killed.

U Aung Win climbed into another house where there

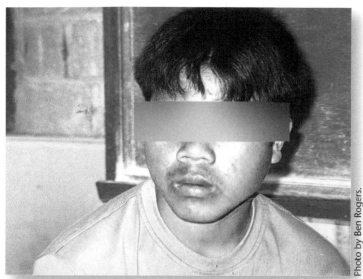

A 15-year-old Shan boy, whose parents had been killed, village destroyed and who was taken as a porter. He was forced to walk long distances, carrying very heavy loads, and was denied food and water for three days. He collapsed from exhaustion, and was beaten unconscious.

Photo by Ben Rogers.

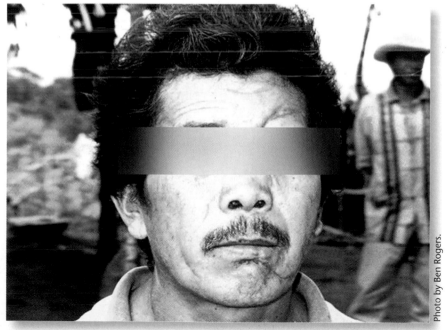

A Shan man, who was used for forced labour. He was beaten in the face.

Photo by Ben Rogers.

Burman child soldiers. The picture of two boys – taken from the street, aged 14 – during military training. They were beaten with steel rods and bamboo sticks.

A Karen village destroyed by SPDC soldiers.

Painting by Karenni child showing his experience of forced labour. The SPDC soldiers stand in the background with their guns. Note his grandfather on the floor being beaten, as is his pregnant aunt as she is forced to carry a heavy load.

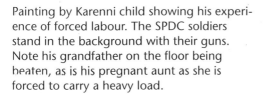

Painting by Karenni child depicting his village being burnt by SPDC soldiers.

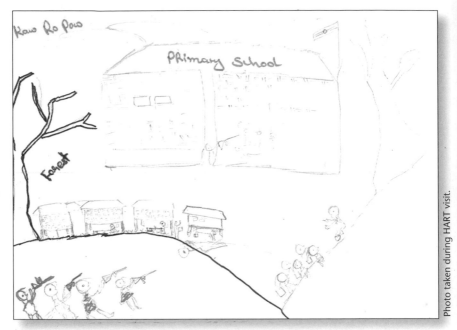

Painting by Karenni girl of the SPDC attack on her primary school. The soldiers are drawn in the bottom left corner, shooting at the fleeing children on the right.

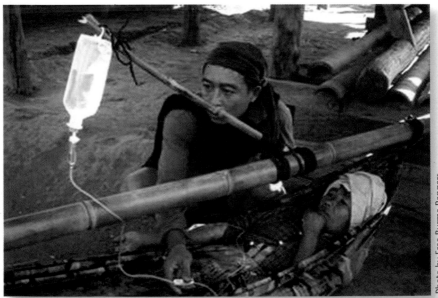

Mobile medical team helping internally displaced peoples in the Karen jungle.

Recently burnt Karen village.

Internally displaced people fleeing from attacks by SPDC troops to avoid massacre or capture and forced labour.

Photos by Free Burma Rangers.

Cover of a report exposing the conscription of women for sexual slavery and other practices of sexual violence by troops of the Burmese military regime in Mon areas. By the Woman and Child Rights Project (Southern Burma), in collaboration with Human Rights Foundation of Monland (Burma), July 2005.

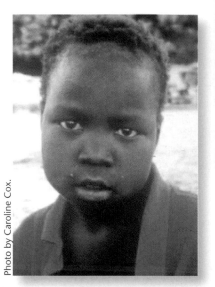

Deng, just returned from slavery. He has just heard that his parents were killed in the slave raid. But he is at least happy that he can now be called by his own name, Deng (the Dinka word for 'rain', which is 'precious'), and not "abd" – or "slave".

Photo by Caroline Cox.

Mr Apin Apin Akot with his rescued family.

Photo by Caroline Cox.

His eldest daughter, Akec Apin Akot

Arec Mawien, an elderly woman standing with Caroline Cox in the charred remains of her compound.

Photo by Caroline Cox.

Photo by Caroline Cox.

Duwar Athar, a Dinka boy aged 6 who was forced to talk in Arabic and was beaten when he didn't.

Photo by Caroline Cox.

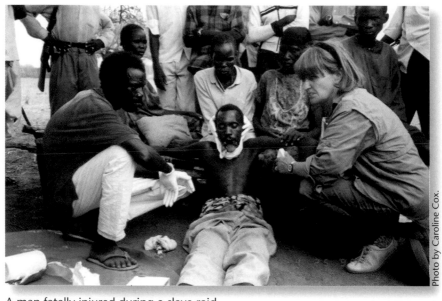

A man fatally injured during a slave raid.

Slaves returning from the north.

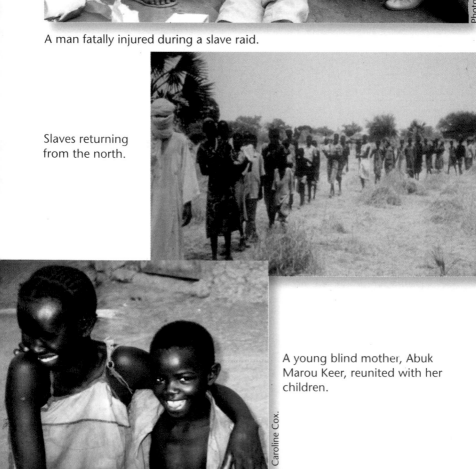

A young blind mother, Abuk Marou Keer, reunited with her children.

Photo by Caroline Cox.

Photo by Caroline Cox.

was only one woman, Mi P-- (about 40 years old), and tried to rape her. When she resisted the rape, he cut Mi P--'s hands, then pointed his knife at her and raped her. After the rape, she lost consciousness owing to heavy blood loss. Then U Aung Win climbed into another house nearby, where there was only a young lady, Mi K-- L-- (about 20 years old), and tried to rape her. When she realised the man was trying to rape her, she cried urgently for help. When he tried to stab her with the knife, she ran out of her house and escaped.

After hearing her cries, the other villagers came to help her. When they found out that the two militiamen had raped some women in the village, they went to help the other two women, Mi P-- and Ma M--. When the villagers arrived, Mi P-- had lost a lot of blood and was in a serious condition. The villagers could not stop the blood flow and they sent her urgently by truck to Yapu village for treatment.

As Ma M-- did not have serious injuries, the villagers did not take her for treatment. Then the villagers arrested the two rapists and sent them to Yapu village, telling the military commanders about the rape cases and violence. However, the rapists did not receive any serious punishment and were simply dismissed from the militia.

(viii) A 20-year-old woman a village in Yei township:
In the second week of Decembe 2003, a woman called Mi A-- L--, 20 years old, was arrested by Captain Hla Khaing and his troop of SPDC Light Infantry Brigade (LIB) No. 586 soon after her father, Nai W--, had been arrested by the commander, Captain Hla Khaing, and accused of being a rebel agent. She was detained by the Burmese soldiers of LIB No. 586 and repeatedly raped by both officers and soldiers. She was mostly gang-raped by the soldiers when they launched a military operation. She was taken from one place to another or one village to another by the soldiers, and they raped her at nighttime. She was not fed with sufficient food and could not sleep for several nights.

Her father disappeared and she never found him. She believes the soldiers killed him.

When she arrived back at her home, she was extremely weak and ill. She said that she had asked the soldiers to kill her instead of raping her, but they kept on raping her. When the soldiers arrived at her home village they let her stay at her home for a while, but when they left for military operations they took her along with them again. In all, she was raped for a total of over two months.

When she was arrested and gang-raped by the Burmese soldiers from LIB No. 586, she was about five to six months pregnant. Her husband had fled to escape arrest and execution by the Burmese soldiers.

According to the latest information, she delivered her baby prematurely after only eight months.

(ix) A 23-year-old unmarried woman, a farmer, from Ye township, Mon State:
At the end of December 2003, SPDC No. 3 Tactical Command, which was conducting a military campaign in southern Ye township, Mon State, ordered the village headmen to send three women daily in rotation to do basic work such as cooking, carrying water, finding firewood, etc., for the military in the daytime and to be raped during the night-time. The women from many households in the village and six villages nearby were forced to send three women every day to the army encampment, where IB No. 299 were temporarily based.

Mi K-- H--, 23, a woman – one of the women who had been raped – said that in the daytime they had to cook meals for the soldiers and carry water for their shower (for the officers, including even low-ranking officers). After having dinner, the soldiers demanded a massage and, when night fell, they raped the women. As the rapes happened at their bases, the women could not resist at all.

The women were alternated with another three women on a rotation basis the next day. This conscription of "comfort women" continued throughout December 2003 and January

2004. Only this woman, Mi K-- H--, confessed that she was raped; the others kept silent about what happened to them during night-time at the military base.

(x) Mi A-- M--, an unmarried 18-year-old woman from Yebyu township, Tenasserim Division:
On August 10, 2004, when a young Mon woman was travelling near her village, she was repeatedly raped by a sergeant from SPDC Light Infantry Brigade No. 406, according to a source close to her. She was travelling with a group of five male villagers from her village to Mae-than-taung village by boat in the morning of August 10.

On the way, an SPDC army sergeant stopped their boat and asked them to approach the riverbank. When the boat stopped, he robbed the passengers, taking all their belongings, including all their valuables, gold and silver.

After the robbery, the sergeant took the woman, Mi A-- M--, with him, letting the boat and other passengers continue. Then he raped the woman for one day and one night. The next morning at about 10am, he brought the young woman to the village. She was immediately taken to the clinic in the village for treatment of injuries. She was in hospital for three days.

On August 12, the sergeant came back to the village and, as the villagers recognised him, they tried to arrest him. He shot at them, injuring some of them. However, the villagers were able to arrest him and tie him up.

The incident happened near the Kanbauk area, where the US company Unocal and the French company Total are involved in the exploitation of gas from the offshore "Yadana" gas field. LIB No. 406 and LIB No. 273 battalions are taking responsibility for the security of the Yadana gas-pipeline area mainly in order to prevent attacks from rebels.

License to Rape: The Burmese Military Regime's Use of Sexual Violence in the Ongoing War in Shan State, by The Shan Human Rights Foundation (SHRF) and The Shan Women's Action Network (SWAN), May 2002

This report details 173 incidents of rape and other forms of sexual violence, involving 625 girls and women, committed by Burmese army troops in Shan State, mostly between 1996 and 2001.

Giving examples of systematic and widespread rape, designed to terrorise and subjugate the Shan people, the report provides strong evidence that war crimes and crimes against humanity, in the form of sexual violence, have occurred and continue to occur in Shan State and that rape is officially condoned as a "weapon of war" against the civilian populations. There appears to be a concerted strategy by the Burmese army troops to rape Shan women as part of their anti-insurgency activities. The incidents described were committed by soldiers from 52 different battalions. 83% of the rapes were committed by officers, usually in front of their own troops. The rapes involved extreme brutality and often torture such as beating, mutilation and suffocation. 25% of the rapes resulted in death, in some incidences with bodies being deliberately displayed to local communities. 61% were gang-rapes; women were raped within military bases, and in some cases they were detained and raped repeatedly for periods of up to four months. Out of the total 173 documented incidents, in only one case was a perpetrator punished by his commanding officer. More commonly, the complainants were fined, detained, tortured or even killed by the military.

Shan women are increasingly vulnerable to rape owing to the increased militarisation and anti-insurgency measures undertaken in Shan State by the Burmese regime, the SPDC. The number of battalions in the state has nearly tripled since 1988. The majority of rape incidents were committed in the areas of Central Shan State, where over 300,000 villagers have been forcibly relocated from their homes since 1996. Many rapes took place when girls or women were caught, usually searching for food, outside the relocation sites. Rapes also occurred when women were being forced to work as porters or do other unpaid work for the military, and when stopped at military checkpoints.

The report also explores some of the physical and mental effects of the rapes on the survivors, who suffered not only from the lack of legal redress for the crimes, but also from the lack of any crisis support. Some survivors faced blame and rejection from their own families and communities. Many of them decided to flee to Thailand after being raped. However, the lack of recognition of Shan refugees in Thailand means these survivors have no protection and no access to humanitarian aid or counselling services. They are thus vulnerable to exploitation and trafficking and are in constant danger of being deported into the hands of their abusers.

Driven Away: Trafficking of Kachin women on the China–Burma border by the Kachin Women's Association of Thailand (KWAT), June 2005 [4]

This report documents aspects of human trafficking that are by-products of the SPDC's catastrophic rule. In Kachin State, the SPDC's record of failed policies has created such acute and widespread poverty that increasing numbers of young people are having to migrate in search of work. Many young women and girls are now disappearing without trace, tricked into the Chinese and Burmese sex industries. Local Kachin researchers conducted interviews in Burma from May to August 2004 in order to ascertain what is happening.

The report is based on 63 verified and suspected trafficking cases, most of which occurred during 2000–2004, involving 85 women and girls, mostly between the ages of fourteen and 20. Testimonies are provided primarily by women and girls who escaped after being trafficked, as well as relatives, people who helped escapees, and others.

In 36 cases, women were offered safe work opportunities and accompanied the recruiters to border towns. They were attracted by the chance to work in order to provide financial support for their families; in some cases, they were specifically seeking money to help to pay for school fees. Those not offered work were taken while looking for work, tricked, or outright abducted.

> *Women taken to China were most often passed on to traffickers at the border to be transported farther by car, bus and/or train for journeys of up to one week in length. Traffickers used deceit, threats, and drugs to confuse and control women en route. Women were transported as far as provinces in north-eastern China for the purpose of being sold as wives to Chinese men. Others were trafficked into the sex industry in Chinese border towns or deeper into south-western Yunnan province. Half of the women involved in those cases have disappeared altogether. Only about 10% of the cases involved domestic trafficking, mostly to karaoke bars and massage parlours in the mining areas of Kachin and Shan State.*[5]

Two examples of individual cases

> (i) *"Yyy" who lives at [address not given for security reasons] arranged that I and my friend would work as waitresses or helpers selling things in Mung Hsu township. It was arranged on September 15, 02 early in the morning at 8am. She said that the payment was good and it was not very hard work. Then we agreed to go and work there. My friend and I were taken on that day by express train from Myitkyina to Mung Hsu. On the train a man came together with us. When we were at Mung Hsu, we did not get work as a waitress or a helper selling things. On September 18 (2002), we were pressured to work as*

prostitutes at a massage parlour. We stayed there about four months. We were threatened in several ways. We could not stand it any more and tried to run away but we were not successful.

Finally, on January 18 (2003), we were taken out from the massage parlour. We did not have enough money to go back to Myitkyina and stayed at a tailoring shop by request. The man who originally took us on the train sent me back to Myitkyina. On January 24, we arrived in Myitkyina at night and he threatened me, saying I shouldn't tell anybody that I had been forced to sell my body. My friend was left behind in Mung Hsu. I did not tell anyone about what had happened to her. I was too confused to tell anybody around me about what had really happened to me. Only finally I revealed what had happened to people, and I was urged to bring charges against our traffickers. On February 3 (2003), I filed a complaint at the police station for trafficking my friend and me into sex work. But no action has been taken. We don't have money so we cannot do anything.[6]

(ii) *My name is "AA", I am 25 years old. I don't have an ID. My father is a retired sailor. My mother is a housewife. The address is [deleted for security]. I stay with my husband. We have one daughter. Now she is seven years old. We stay with my husband's parents.*

Six years ago, I, my sister and another woman were sold to China... I have only just returned. I don't know where my sister is or whether she is alive or not. The other woman is now the wife of a Chinese man. Now she has already got one child. One day, two people who lived in Mye Myit came and talked about getting a housekeeping job, which would earn 5,000 kyat per month. If the boss liked your ability, you would get more. When I asked my husband, he also agreed so I prepared to go and do this job. They gave me 3,000 kyat as an advance. I consulted with my mother and I called my sister to join. On 8 June

1997 they came and picked us up. Then at Wai Maw ferry site, they handed us over to someone else. We rode a motorboat. When we reached Wai Maw we were handed over to a strange man. The woman and the man took us to China and sold us.

He was a Lisu and the woman was his minor wife. They told us they would take us to Laiza. We had never been to Laiza. They said that the journey would take two hours but it took many days. When we asked them where they were taking us, they told us not to ask so many questions, and that if we wanted to go back we could. We couldn't go back, as we had no money to return and we were very frightened. So we just had to do whatever they said. One woman (I don't know her name) took us to one of the houses by the ferry dock. There one man was waiting for us. That man and woman took us to the station where we could take a bus to Laiza. We all rode on a bus to Laiza. On 8 June 1997, at 6pm we reached Laiza. When we reached Laiza, we arrived at what looked like a guest house, and we were locked into a room. Soon the man and woman came to call us and then we went to take a bath. After that we ate some food. We slept in Laiza for one night.

The next day at 8am five of us rode together in a car. In the afternoon we reached Yae Chin town. We reached there at 3pm and then we continued to travel by bus. On the way, we arrived at a town. We five people slept in only one room of a guest house. Next day, all five people continued our journey by car. At 11pm we continued by train. After three days, at 6am we reached Nan Kyin railway station. From that station, we rode again in a bus and then reached Tong Shyi village.

In Tong Shyi village, we stayed at one house. Many people came and looked at us. I think that they had been told in advance about us. Men chose us. At that time my sister was young and stoutly built, so they chose her first.

When my sister protested, the Lisu man hit her face and kicked her. My sister was crying, but she had to follow the man who had come to take her because she was so afraid. My sister was very strong-minded. She ran away from the man three times. So they let the third woman (from Yan Gyi Aung) take the place of my sister.

Then they sent my sister somewhere very far away. Since that day I haven't seen or met with my sister. I don't know whether she is alive or not. I have had no information about her. One man chose me, and called me away, so I followed him. His legs were crippled as a result of a wrong injection when he was young. I stayed with him and we got one son. I stayed six years with him in Kyau Tsut Du Yit village, Nan Kyin province. My son's name is Shin Yit. Now he is five years old.

In March 2003, I asked the Chinese man if I could go back home just for a short while. When I reached home, I learned that my sister hadn't come back yet so I went to Laiza to look for her. I noticed the Lisu man sitting in front of me. When I saw him, I remembered what had happened. I was filled with resentment. I was so angry it made my heart beat fast. I pretended to forget my ID and I told the car driver that I needed to go and get my ID and asked him to drive to my mother's house. When we arrived home, I reported the man to the headman and he was arrested. When we asked him where my sister was, he told me that I shouldn't speak to him like that as he could arrest me. He said he used to be a KIA soldier.

On 2 March 2004, my mother reported what had happened to the local SPDC headman and then the Intelligence and Police caught him. We knew that No.2 Police Station had sent the records to the court already. In the court, the Lisu man and his relatives shouted at me so I felt sad and afraid. I was already suffering from a heart condition. Eventually the court hearing was postponed. A teacher and someone who seemed to be her husband from

Nan Kyi village came and asked me how much money I wanted for compensation, and to reach a settlement with the accused. She also said that the accused was a relative of her husband and if I didn't reach a settlement with him, they would press charges against me. The teacher came and negotiated with me to accept compensation, but I wouldn't accept any money. One of the police, a relative of the Lisu man (who is also a policeman), said to me: "What are you doing? Do you want to go to jail?" I was very afraid and went to tell my grandmother.[7]

Let the Victims of Forced Labour Speak

The SPDC routinely uses forced labour, targeting the ethnic national groups in particular for this extremely arduous, harrowing and often dangerous work. The frequency with which people are required to interrupt their normal activities is often so disruptive that they cannot make a living. For example, they may be taken from cultivating their crops at critical times, so they lose their harvest and the food on which their survival depends.

In some cases, the period of forced labour brings extra hazards: some who have to serve as porters for SPDC soldiers are forced to walk ahead of the troops, as human minesweepers; many perish or suffer severe injuries when stepping on mines. For women, as we have seen, the enforced time away from their homes may incur not only hard labour by day but also subjection to sexual assault at night.

Elderly people may have to carry loads of rice or ammunition, weighing up to 30kg (over 60lbs) from dawn until dusk. If they walk slowly, or succumb to fatigue, they are beaten; some die as a result of beatings or exhaustion.

The policy of forced labour has been well documented.[8] We now hear the voices of some of those who have been subjected to it, describing the reality.

(i) Naw KSP, a woman aged 36, from a village in No. 2 District, Karenni State. She fled abroad because she did not want to be a forced porter:

> *I have already been used as a porter by the Burma Army three times, for several days at a time. I had to carry 16kg bags of rice, walking from 3am until dusk each day. From 3am until noon we were given no food. In the afternoon the soldiers would sometimes give us rice and yellow beans, with fish paste. If we grew tired and stopped to rest, or faint, we would be beaten by the soldiers. Villagers took turns to provide porters for the troops but, on average, from 20 households, at least five porters were taken every month.*

(ii) A 24-year-old woman and her mother, aged 55, from a village in No. 2 District, Karenni state. In 1996, their village and seven other villages had been relocated to the town of Mawchi and the villagers used as forced porters. In 2000 they returned to their village to find that everything had been burnt down. The Burma Army again demanded porters and one of the daughters of the family had to go to the front line to carry ammunition for the soldiers. She was extremely traumatised, and on her return the family decided they had to flee into the jungle to avoid further forced labour. They had to carry their father, who was ill and paralysed; he died in the jungle in 2003. Living in the jungle, they survived by eating bamboo, vegetables, rice, birds and mice. Many of them became sick with fevers and diarrhoea. They eventually fled across the border to a camp in Thailand.

(iii) A mother with three children, aged eight, thirteen and fourteen, from a village near Mawchi, in Karenni State. They left Mawchi because SPDC soldiers forced them to serve as porters – or demanded money, which they could not pay. Therefore, her husband had to work as a porter. He was used as a human minesweeper, forced to walk ahead of SPDC soldiers. He was killed by a mine and she never saw him again.

She was pregnant at the time with her younger daughter, who was born after her husband was killed. She crossed the border to come to Thailand, because the SPDC were very close to their home in Burma and they demanded forced labour for two to three months. She said it was very hard to work on the farm under those conditions; also, the children could not attend school in Mawchi because she could not pay the fees. She concluded our interview thus:

> If we stay in Burma, the SPDC come to force us to work; they burn our homes and villages and therefore we can't stay there. If we return to Burma, the SPDC soldiers will kill us – or force the local people to do so.

(iv) A 35-year-old married woman with two children from a village in Karen State:

> My husband died or was killed when acting as a forced porter for the SPDC. I was never told how he died or allowed to see his body, but was merely told he had been buried in the forest. At the time of his death, my two sons were aged seven and one year old. My husband, a rice farmer, had had to work many times as a porter, usually for two to three weeks at a time. Portering could only be avoided or deferred by paying the local SPDC commander. Porters would all have to provide their own food, work for nine to ten hours per day and had to carry loads of 50–60kg, Those unable to work such hours or to carry such loads were firstly beaten, usually with rifles; then, if they still could or would not comply, they were shot. I had to do portering duties twice after my husband's death, leaving my children with relatives while I was away. There were about 100 porters in my group and about 70% of them were women. We started work at 8am and had a fifteen-minute break at midday and then worked until 4pm. We slept on mats on the jungle floor and soldiers would come at night and take any women they chose for the night (I was not one of them). My task was to carry rocks

and stones to build a road and a railway. When my husband was alive we used to have cows and chickens and pigs, but the soldiers came and took everything. I feel safe and secure in Thailand – but I want to go back and live in peace in my own village.

(v) A 30-year-old Buddhist woman from Karen State:

My village had about 100 houses and I think that all the villagers were Buddhists. My husband had been used many times as a porter and had become very weak and exhausted. SPDC troops would often come into the village and steal food, sometimes two or three times weekly. I think this was because there was an SPDC barracks near my village. All the men and women in the village had to do portering duties, mainly carrying ammunition and food for the soldiers. In addition, porters would have to provide and carry all their own food. I would estimate the loads to be between 40 and 50kg per person. SPDC troops would often call all the villagers together, harangue them and accuse them of harbouring rebel soldiers. The village leaders and elders were picked out, beaten and cut with machete knives. Just before I left in September one such elder had been cut all over his body and had bled to death. About ten people from my village were killed in the last year. In addition, about once or twice a month, small groups of soldiers would enter the village, select one of the girls and take her into the forest, where she would be repeatedly gang-raped. The girls were told that if they complained, the headman of the village would be disciplined and beaten. If villagers resisted the soldiers' demands, they were simply shot. All the villagers were anxious and afraid. Both Buddhists and Christians suffer human rights abuses by the SPDC. I would say that women are generally treated worse than men.

(vi) A 35-year-old widow from Karen State:

My husband died in 1991, following an infected fish bite on his foot, which was untreated, resulting in generalised infection and death three months later. As he had been required to perform portering duties prior to his death and was unable to fulfil them, the SPDC came three months after his death and took my ten-year-old son to be a porter instead. As he was a slight lad, he was unable to carry the loads and the soldiers beat him to death. My remaining son was one year old at the time. He is now eight years old. I was never allowed to see the body of my son or to bury him. After my son's death, I was then required to act as a porter, leaving my baby son with relatives. During the time I worked I saw dozens of other porters beaten and physically attacked and abused by soldiers. I would estimate that, out of my group of 100, about 15–20 were killed, either by beating or shooting.

(vii) A 30-year-old woman with a husband and three children, from Karen State:

There was no food in my village, nor was there any medical help available when villagers got sick. My husband was forced to be a porter twice every month for between one and three weeks, which left him no time to till his fields or grow rice. For ten hours a day he had to carry loads of small arms and ammunition, weighing around 60kg, which were for use against his own people. I also had to work once a month as a porter, carrying both the heavy load and my baby on my back. Burmese troops would frequently come into my village to steal food and animals. Members of the army told the village leaders they had to produce more food to feed the soldiers as that was their only source of food.

(viii) A 24-year-old woman from Karen State:

> *The Burmese troops used to come to my village and demand that the villagers perform porter duty or pay 300 kyats. We were scared of them because they would beat us, so we would go with them. On one occasion my husband refused to go, and the soldiers beat him with a solid wooden baton. I was taken as a porter a total of eight times. We would be taken three to four days at a time. I had to carry things such as ammunition, food, army rations and the soldiers' belongings or utensils. The loads were very heavy, I would estimate that I had to carry about 30 kilos and I am very small and slight, so it was very hard work. I also had to build trenches for the army. Sometimes we would have to work in the day and sometimes at night. If I was slow they would beat me. I was not given any food and was always hungry. I often ran away. I knew that if we were caught running away we would be shot, but it was not always difficult to escape. I had to come to Thailand because I did not have any food. I could not afford to pay the porter taxes and it was difficult to go to the farm. The soldiers took our food, so there was not enough left for us to eat. It took five days to get here by foot.*

Child Soldiers

Burma has the notorious reputation of maintaining the highest number of child soldiers in the world today. It is estimated that 70,000 boys have been conscripted, many having been abducted while going about their daily lives, sent straight to military training and then out to serve with SPDC troops, often in areas of active conflict. They do not have an opportunity to tell their families what has happened to them, so parents do not know where their sons have gone.

The report "My Gun was as Tall as Me: Child Soldiers in Burma"[9] claims that the overwhelming majority of Burma's child soldiers are found in the national army, the Tatmadaw Kyi, which forcibly recruits children as young as eleven.

Summaries of interviews cited in this report are entirely consistent with the conversations we have had with some boys who had escaped from the Tatmadaw and fled to relative safety in Thailand. These interviews, typical of many others, are quoted from "My Gun was as Tall as Me".[10]

> (i) *On the way there was a checkpoint. The police stopped the car and checked ID cards. I couldn't show one. I was too young to have an ID card... The police said, "You'll have to go to jail for six years for not having an ID card." Then they sent me to the police station and put me in the leg stocks. But I could pull my feet out because the holes in the stocks were too big for my feet, so two policemen guarded me. They kept saying, "You have to decide. You can join the army or go to jail." And then they gave me time to think. They could see I was only eleven, but if the police give a boy to the army they can get pocket money from the army: 3,000 kyat and two tins of rice. They gave me from 8am until the afternoon to decide. I didn't want to go to jail for six years, so I agreed to join the army.*

(ii) Khin Maung Than, recruited into the Burma army in 1999 at age eleven:

> *When we arrived [at the recruit holding centre] the soldiers asked us, "Would you like to join the army or would you like to go home?" Many of us said we'd like to go home. Then they took the 30 or 40 of us who'd said that, stripped us naked, put us in the lock-up and gave us just a tiny bit of rice... There were about 60 of us in a room the same size as this one [four to five metres square]... I don't think any were over 18. There were ten children who were just thirteen years old. The youngest was my friend, who was eleven. He often cried because he didn't get enough*

food, and then he was beaten by the guards. I also cried often because I didn't want to join the army. I was beaten twice a day for crying... We couldn't sleep. There were also rats and ants in the room... For a toilet they'd dug a hole in the ground and it had a wooden cover over it... There was a terrible smell... Some of my friends were crying... Two or three boys got sick and died.

(iii) Than Aung, recruited into the Burma army in 1997 at age fourteen:

The section leader ordered us to take cover and open fire. There were seven of us, and seven or ten of the enemy. I was too afraid to look, so I put my face in the ground and shot my gun up at the sky. I was afraid their bullets would hit my head. I fired two magazines, about 40 rounds. I was afraid that if I didn't fire, the section leader would punish me... The corporal beat the soldiers, the sergeant beat the corporal, and sometimes the 2nd lieutenant beat the sergeant. It's always like this in the army.

We do not give any details of the boys whom we interviewed, as they are in an inherently vulnerable situation. Abducted from bus stops or the cinema, aged eleven or twelve, they were forcibly conscripted. After a brief period of training, they were sent to the front line in areas of conflict with the ethnic national armies of the Karen or Karenni people. They were badly treated, often hungry, and very unhappy about their families not knowing what had happened to them. They said they could not go home, or even contact their families, because to do so might incur reprisals. They also said that they were deeply unhappy about the brutality they were forced to inflict on innocent civilians.

One boy said that the "last straw" which made him feel he would anything to escape was having to beat elderly people who were forced to work as porters. He said he imagined he was beating his grandparents – and that was so intolerable, he just had to run away.

Conclusion

Having made at least a dozen visits to the Thai–Burmese borderlands and two visits to the Chin people in the India–Burma borderlands, with different groups from diverse organisations, my colleagues and I have, between us, records of several hundred interviews with people who have been subjected to the range of gross violations of human rights detailed above.

The cumulative evidence is overwhelming. It is clear that the SPDC has systematic policies for the subjugation of ethnic national groups. These include forced labour, requiring men, women and sometimes children to carry very heavy loads for the army, with virtually no rest or respite. Those who fall by the wayside are at risk of being beaten and killed. Some have to serve as human minesweepers.

The frequency of the requirement to work as forced labour is such that it is often difficult for civilians to support themselves and their family. It is possible to pay bribes to escape portering duties, but most people cannot afford the money required. Women may be doubly vulnerable – not only to having to carry heavy burdens by day, but also to the additional burden of sexual exploitation by night.

Sexual exploitation, humiliation and the systematic use of rape as a weapon of war are also well and widely documented. The abduction and forcible conscription into the army of tens of thousands of boys is also widely known.

Despite numerous reports by the ILO[11] and various human-rights organisations[12], the SPDC continues to subject its citizens to these practices with impunity. Although the SPDC has been subjected to pressure by some members of the international community, the suffering of the people continues unabated – and is even escalating in scale and intensity.

PART 2

Slavery Past and Present

Introduction
What is Slavery?
Definitions, Distinctions and International Conventions

The League of Nations was set up in the aftermath of the First World War. In 1919 they: *"...affirmed their intention of securing the complete suppression of slavery in all its forms and of the slave trade by land and sea."*[1] In due course this led to the Slavery Convention – signed in September 1926 and coming into force in March 1927 – which sought to secure the abolition of slavery and the slave trade, which were defined thus:

> *(1) Slavery is the status or condition of a person over whom any or all of the powers attaching to the right of ownership are exercised.*

> *(2) The slave trade includes all acts involved in the capture, acquisition or disposal of a person with intent to reduce him to slavery; all acts involved in the acquisition of a slave with a view to selling or exchanging him; all acts of disposal by sale or exchange of a slave acquired with a view to being sold or exchanged, and, in general, every act of trade or transport in slaves.*[2]

The United Nations was set up following the Second World War, and in 1948 agreed the Universal Declaration of Human Rights (UDHR). Article 4 guarantees that: *"No one shall be held in slavery or servitude; slavery and the slave trade shall be prohibited in all their forms."*

In 1998, the United Nations established a Working Group on Contemporary Forms of Slavery (WGCFS) to investigate the nature and extent of different forms of slavery in the modern world. The High Commissioner for Human Rights in his opening statement to WCGFS stated:

> *Slavery and its prohibition is enshrined in international treaties and in the 1948 Universal Declaration of Human Rights (UDHR) of which the international community is actually commemorating the 50th anniversary ... but still, slavery is not dead. It continues to be reported in a wide range of forms: traditional chattel slavery, bonded labour, serfdom, child labour, migrant labour, domestic labour, forced labour and slavery for ritual or religious purposes.*[3]

Although slavery has taken new and diverse forms, the essential criterion remains as it has throughout history: ownership of or control over another person's life, associated with coercion and restriction of movement. Therefore, someone can be deemed to be in a state of enforced servitude or slavery if he or she is forced to work without payment or rights and cannot leave without explicit permission.

In Chapter Five we will discuss and document these modern forms of slavery in more detail. But first we will briefly consider the long history of slavery through the ages.

CHAPTER FOUR

Slavery Through the Ages

Slavery of one kind or another – in which some human beings deprived others of many or most of the rights held by the free – has occurred throughout most of recorded history. Slaves were typically the object rather than the subject of the law.

Ancient Mediterranean Civilisations

Most of these civilisations had slaves and were dependent on them. But slavery:

> ...*seems to have been especially important in the development of two of the world's major civilizations, Western (including ancient Greece and Rome) and Islamic.*[1]

The two main kinds of slavery were domestic or household slavery, which was fairly common, and productive slavery, usually in mines and plantations.

All the ancient Greek city-states permitted slavery but the laws differed greatly from state to state. The most famous city-state was Athens. During its classical period, from the fifth to the third century BC, slaves made up about a third of the population, with many employed in the Laurium silver mines.

The Athenian slave society came to an end after the defeat of Athens by Philip II of Macedon in 338 BC.

Ancient Rome was the next major slave society – from about the second century BC to the fourth century AD. As the

Roman Empire grew, Rome changed from a society of small farmers to a major military power. During Rome's waves of expansion, it acquired many slaves by conquest, who mainly worked in farming the olives and grapes that made Rome prosperous. At some periods as many as 30% of the population were slaves, but the practice gradually died out as many were converted into "coloni" or serfs, who had more rights than slaves but were still tied to the land.

The Early Years of Islam

Slavery has been associated with many Islamic societies for most of the 1,400 years of Islam's existence, ranging from Arabia and surrounding countries at the heart of Islam to North Africa in the west and what is now Pakistan and Indonesia in the east.[2] Moreover:

> *Some Islamic states, such as the Ottoman Empire, the Crimean Khanate, and the Sokoto caliphate, must be termed slave societies because slaves there were very important numerically as well as a focus of the polities' energies.*[3]

This is no accident, since the Koran itself regulates the practice of slavery and thus implicitly accepts it, while Muhammad and some of his Companions owned slaves and obtained more by conquest.[4]

The Koran recognises the basic inequality between master and slave and the rights of the former over the latter.[5] It also recognises concubinage.[6] Before Islam, slavery and slaves, who were mainly captured in wars, were well known throughout the Mediterranean and Arabia. Azumah argues that:

> *...this pre-Islamic practice, like many others, is accepted in classical Muslim traditions as a matter of course. In the Qur'an, the periphrasis "those whom you right hand possess" is used more frequently to refer to slaves than "abid,*

plural of 'abd, the Arabic term for slave. In the language of the Qur'an, slaves are a legitimate property for Muslims.[7]

The Koran condemns the use of female slaves as prostitutes but instead allows Muslim men to have lawful sexual relations with an unlimited number of his female slaves. The Koran also recommends but does not require kindness to slaves and allows their liberation by purchase (manumission).

In short:

slavery as a practice is... not condemned in either the Qur'an or hadith. If anything at all the practice is endorsed with modifications and stipulations aimed at regulating and mitigating possible abuses...[8]

However, these stipulations may not reflect what actually happens.

Yet, as Bernard Lewis points out, there is a remarkable lack of scholarly work on Islamic slavery:

For the central Islamic lands, despite the subject's importance in virtually every area and period, a list of serious scholarly monographs on slavery – in law, in doctrine, or in practice – could be printed on a single page. The documentation for a study on Islamic slavery is almost endless; its exploration has barely begun.[9]

This lack of attention to Islamic slavery is in stark contrast to the many thousands of studies made by European and American scholars of slavery in the ancient world, in medieval Europe and in the Americas.

The revolt of the Zanj (869–883 AD)

One little-known example of slavery in early Islam is the existence of considerable numbers of black slaves – some sources say as many as 3 million – working on plantations clearing the swamps, building canals and growing cotton and sugar under the Abbasid caliphate in Baghdad in the ninth century. Most

came from the Zanzibar coast of Africa and were known as the
Zanj. In 869 AD they revolted and were not finally defeated for
nearly fifteen years, until 883 AD.[10]

The Zanj revolt marked the end of plantation slavery in
the Islamic world, but other forms of slavery continued under
the Abbasids and elsewhere.

Medieval Europe

During the eastward expansion of Europeans from the sixth to
the tenth centuries, a great many people of Slavonic origin
were captured as slaves. So many Slavs were enslaved that it
gave rise to the word "slave". Later in medieval Europe the
slaves became landless serfs who had more rights than chattel
slaves but less than most other Europeans at the time. Many
Slavs were also enslaved towards the end of this period in the
Middle East and other Muslim lands.

Slave soldiers in the Middle East and elsewhere

Pipes describes in detail the use of slaves as soldiers within
Islam for over a thousand years – from the ninth to the nineteenth centuries – in locations all over the Muslim world, from
central Africa in the south to central Asia in the north and
from Spain in the west to Bengal in the east. Within Muslim
armies, slaves:

> ...served both as soldiers and as officers, then often
> acquired pre-eminent roles in administration, politics,
> and all aspects of public affairs. The systematic use of
> slaves as soldiers constituted the single most distinctive
> feature of Islamic public life in premodern times...

Moreover:

> ...the premier dynasties of Islam nearly all depended on
> military slaves. These are the governments which governed
> the greatest areas, lasted the longest, and most influenced

the development of Islamic institutions...of seventeen pre-eminent dynasties... all but one relied on military slaves.[11]

In summary:

...in contrast to the erratic employment of slaves as soldiers by non-Muslims, military slavery in Islam served as a nearly universal tool of statecraft. Elsewhere, slaves fought as emergency forces, personal retainers, auxiliaries, or cannon fodder; only Muslims used them in large numbers on a regular basis as professional soldiers.[12]

One example were the slave soldiers known as Mamelukes[13] – members of one of the armies of slaves that won political control of several Muslim states during the Middle Ages. The use of Mamelukes in Muslim armies was common as early as the ninth century. The result frequently was that the slaves used their military power to seize control over the political authorities. The most dramatic example was the Mameluke dynasty, which ruled Egypt and Syria from 1250 to 1517 and whose descendants in Egypt remained an important political force during the Ottoman occupation (1517–1798).

Africa and the intra-African Slave Trade

Azumah describes how:

the trans-Saharan slave trade increased in volume during the eighteenth and nineteenth centuries. Ottoman rulers in league with Muslim Bornu transported large numbers of slaves across the Sahara into the then Ottoman Empire. Many eyewitness accounts talk of substantial loss of lives during the raids and journeys into servitude.[14]

We cannot describe these events here in any detail, but will return to the topic in a later section.[15] But what we can say is that where slavery has been abolished or diminished in Islamic societies, this has almost always been at the instigation of or under pressure from colonial European powers.

In summary, according to the Encyclopedia Britannica:

Slaves have been owned in black Africa throughout recorded history. In many areas there were large-scale slave societies, while in others there were slave-owning societies. Slavery was practised everywhere even before the rise of Islam, and black slaves exported from Africa were widely traded throughout the Islamic world. Approximately 18,000,000 Africans were delivered into the Islamic trans-Saharan and Indian Ocean slave trades between 650 and 1905.[16]

The Atlantic Slave Trade

The Atlantic slave trade was an enormous commercial and maritime undertaking lasting nearly four hundred years – from about 1500 to 1870. About 10 million black slaves were taken from Africa to ports in America. The main carriers were the Portuguese (about 4.5 million), the British (about 2.5 million), the Spanish (about 1.5 million) and the French (over 1 million). The slaves first went mainly to Brazil and the West Indies (about 4 million each) and the Spanish empire (about 2.5 million), and then to British and US North America (about half a million). They worked mainly on plantations – sugar (about 5 million), coffee (about 2 million) and cotton (about half a million), as domestic servants (about 2 million), or into mines (about 1 million).

At the peak of the Atlantic slave trade – in the 1780s – the English and French were each carrying about 40,000 slaves a year. The slaves came from many regions of Africa including Angola, Ashanti, Benin, Congo, Dahomey, Loango, Madagascar and Mozambique, and were exchanged for textiles, copper and iron bars, guns, brandy, rum, cowrie shells and numerous other items.[17]

The Atlantic and intra-African slave trades were linked:

The relationship between African and New World slavery was highly complementary. African slave owners demanded primarily women and children for labour and lineage incorporation and tended to kill males because they were troublesome and likely to flee. The transatlantic trade, on the other hand, demanded primarily adult males for labour and thus saved from certain death many adult males who otherwise would have been slaughtered outright by their African captors.[18]

Abolition of the Slave Trade and Slavery

As we have seen in Chapter One, abolition was the achievement of William Wilberforce and his allies, who first – in 1807 – abolished the slave trade in the British Empire and then – in 1833 – succeeded in finally abolishing slavery, again in the British Empire.

The Acts of the British Parliament did not, in themselves, eliminate either the slave trade or slavery. But the example set by Britain, together with the power of the British navy in the nineteenth century, made a major contribution to the elimination of first the slave trade and then slavery in the other European empires of the nineteenth and early twentieth centuries. However, even in the British Empire, slavery was such an entrenched institution that the mere act of abolition was insufficient to change the settled practices of generations or even centuries.

In the Americas – and in the United States in particular – the balance in the Senate of pro- and anti-slavery states was maintained until the turbulence of the Civil War (1860–1865). President Abraham Lincoln initially intended that the war should maintain the Union of the United States but, as it ground on, he decided to make emancipation of the slaves a major plank of his policy.

Lincoln's Emancipation Proclamation of January 1,

1863 had initially only symbolic importance but the 13th Amendment to the Constitution in December 1865 in due course led to the emancipation of all slaves in the union, although genuine social equality in some states was not achieved until the civil-rights movement of the middle of the twentieth century.

The twentieth century has also seen the re-emergence of religiously legitimated slavery in the Islamist militaristic jihad in Sudan.

And now, in the twenty-first century, we are faced with both the persistence of slavery within the Islamic world and the emergence of new, or the re-emergence of old, forms of slavery – chattel slavery, debt bondage, forced labour, sexual slavery and human trafficking – in very many parts of the world. We turn to these developments in the next chapter.

But before doing so let us not forget that:

> ...it was Europe... that first decided to set the slaves free: at home, then in the colonies, and finally in all the world. Western technology made slavery unnecessary; Western ideas made it intolerable. There have been many slaveries, but there has been only one abolition, which eventually shattered even the rooted and ramified slave systems of the Old World.[19]

CHAPTER FIVE

Contemporary Slavery – Variations on the Theme

In this chapter we briefly review the main types of slavery in the modern world – chattel slavery, debt bondage, forced labour, sex slavery and human trafficking.

Chattel Slavery

This is the classic form, in which slave owners maintain ownership of human beings through force and violence.

Contemporary examples are found in Sudan and Mauritania. In Sudan, the National Islamic Front regime (NIF), which took power by military coup in 1989, declared militaristic jihad against all who oppose it – Muslims and traditional believers as well as Christians.

As we saw in Chapter One, slavery has been one of the weapons of this jihad. Although some forms of inter-tribal or inter-community raids, associated with abductions of civilians, had been a feature of life in certain areas in Sudan, the situation changed in the early 1990s when the NIF regime explicitly encouraged their jihad warriors (mujahidin) and local tribesmen (murahaleen) to engage in slave raids, providing them with weapons and logistical support. Thereafter, massive slave raids took place, especially in the borderlands between southern and northern Sudan, with thousands of civilians, mainly women and children, being abducted into slavery.

According to the US State Department's *Trafficking in Persons Report*, published in June 2005:

> *Sudan is a source country for women and children trafficked for the purposes of forced labor and sexual exploitation. Sudanese boys are trafficked to the Middle East, particularly the United Arab Emirates and Kuwait, for use as camel jockeys. The Lord's Resistance Army (LRA), a Ugandan rebel group, continued to abduct children in war-torn northern Uganda for use as cooks, porters, sex slaves, and combat soldiers. Although Ugandan military offensives during the year significantly reduced LRA numbers, the group continued to conduct operations involving forced child soldiers from camps in southern Sudan. The vast majority of the trafficking within Sudan, however, has involved abductions of largely women in the western and southern regions of the country, territories outside the central government's complete control because of ongoing political, cultural, and civil conflict. In the Sudanese context, inter-tribal abductions are a by-product of various, complex civil wars waged over the past two decades.*
>
> *Abduction, a traditional but dormant cultural practice, was revived with the resurgence of the north/south civil war in 1983. The Dinka Chiefs' Committee estimates that, during these years of civil war and resulting inter-tribal warfare, 14,000 Dinka women and children were abducted by two other tribes (Missiriya and Rezeigat). An additional 3,500 abductions reportedly occurred in SPLA-held regions. Victims frequently became part of the abductor's tribal family, with many women marrying into the new tribe; however, some victims of abduction were used for forced domestic labor and/or sexual exploitation. Due to the ongoing peace process and the cessation of conflict in the south, abductions in the region have significantly decreased; during the year, there were no known cases of new abductions in the south.*

The regions of Southern Darfur and Western Kordofan remained embroiled in a separate bitter conflict, in which numerous rapes, atrocities, and abductions were reported to have taken place during the year. During the reporting period, janjaweed militias that have been supported by the Government of Sudan subjected civilians to grievous human rights and alleged trafficking-related abuses. The lack of security in the Darfur region impeded the ability to gather further information on these reports, which is of grave concern. Women, after being raped, were sometimes mutilated or abducted for further sexual exploitation. Some children may also have been abducted, mostly to care for looted livestock.[1]

Slavery in Mauritania

Another report from the year 2000 argues that, in Mauritania, chattel slavery of black Africans has never ended. It started in the thirteenth century when:

> *...Arab-Berber raiders descended upon Mauritania's indigenous African tribes, abducted women and children, and then bred a new caste of slaves.*
>
> *The raids had long ceased by 2000, but the bedein (white Arab masters), who disdained physical work, still hold haratine (black African slaves) as property. Haratine mothers do not own their own children; they are instead passed down through their master's estate. Slaves are bought and sold, given as wedding gifts, and traded for camels, trucks, or guns. The enslaved perform domestic work, haul water, and shepherd cattle.*[2]

A clandestine anti-slavery group (El Hor – literally "The Free") organised by former slaves estimates that current numbers of haratine in Mauritania may be about one million with hundreds of thousands more in the bordering countries of Mali and Senegal.

Debt Bondage

Perhaps the most widespread form of modern slavery, debt bondage is most commonly associated with widespread, crippling poverty. In some desperate circumstances, families are forced to offer the labour of family members as collateral against a financial loan. In countries where there is a massive population boom, high unemployment and acute poverty, families may be driven to take this measure of last resort. Once trapped, it is very hard to escape from this kind of bondage. Their predicament is exacerbated by inflated interest rates, so that debts may be inherited, passing from one generation to the next. This type of slavery is found in countries such as India, Pakistan, Nepal and Bangladesh. As many as 15–20 million people may be trapped in this kind of slavery today.[3]

Forced Labour

Coercion to work involuntarily – without payment, freedom to leave, or recognition of any rights – takes various forms in the modern world. The International Labour Organisation (ILO) defines "forced labour" as "all work or service which is extracted from any person under the menace of any penalty and for which the said person has not offered himself voluntarily". There are some exceptions, such as conditions relating to military service, legally convicted offenders and those involved with some emergency situations. These exceptions are justified by the fact that people in these situations are protected by certain formal, legal rights.

The ILO defines slavery as a form of forced labour and claims that child labour amounts to forced labour in which the child's work is exacted from the family. An ILO Report in 2005 claimed that about 12.3 million people are in forced labour worldwide; about 2.4 million of them are victims of trafficking, and their labour generates profits of over $30bn. Forced labour is a global problem, in all regions and types of economy. The largest numbers are in poor Asian countries and Latin America, but there are more than 350,000 cases in the industrialised world.[4]

The following tables and diagrams – derived from data in the ILO Report – graphically illustrate the types, numbers, locations and profits from forced labour around the world today.

As we saw earlier, one dramatic example of forced labour is found in Burma (Myanmar), where the oppressive SDPC regime uses systematic policies of forced labour. It tends in particular to exploit ethnic tribal groups in this way. There are numerous well-documented reports of policies of systematic compulsion by SPDC officials to inflict forced labour on the Karen, Karenni and Shan peoples in eastern Burma as well as the Chin and Kachin peoples living in the north-west. Typically, in Karen and Karenni states, SPDC soldiers will move into a district, summon the local leader and require him to allocate a certain number of his local people for labour, for a specified period of time. Conditions under which they have to work and live are notoriously harsh. Required to provide and carry their own food, the villagers have to exist on meagre rations of rice and water, working from dawn until dusk, with minimum rest. Even elderly people and pregnant women have to work as porters, carrying heavy loads (30kg) of ammunition or rice for soldiers, who beat them mercilessly if they show signs of fatigue.

Others may be used as human minesweepers, forced to walk ahead of columns of SPDC troops. Many have been killed or maimed by treading on mines in this way. Those injured are usually just left to die. Testimonies of some of these victims of forced labour in Burma are found earlier in the book (see Chapter Three).

Again, according to the US State Department's *Trafficking in Persons Report*, published in June 2005:

Table 1 Forced Labour – Types and Numbers

Types	Numbers	%
State/Military	2,490,000	20
Private Economic	7,810,000	64
Private Sexual	1,390,000	11
Mixed	610,000	5
Total	12,300,000	100

Forced labour – Types and Numbers

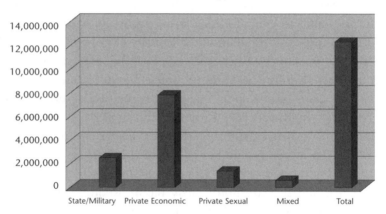

Types of Forced Labour

Table 2 Forced Labour by Region

Region	Total numbers	Trafficked Numbers	Trafficking Profits ($ Million)
Asia & Pacific	9,490,000	1,360,000	9,704
Latin America/Caribbean	1,320,000	250,000	1,348
Sub-Saharan Africa	660,000	130,000	159
Industrialised Countries	360,000	270,000	15,513
Middle East/North Africa	260,000	230,000	1,508
Transition Countries	210,000	200,000	3,422
Total	12,300,000	2,440,000	31,654

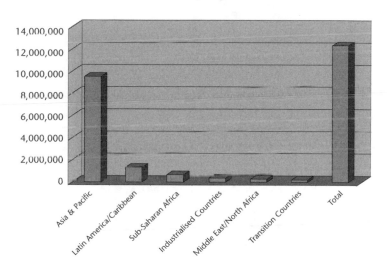

Forced labour by Region – Total numbers

Forced labour by Region – Trafficked Numbers

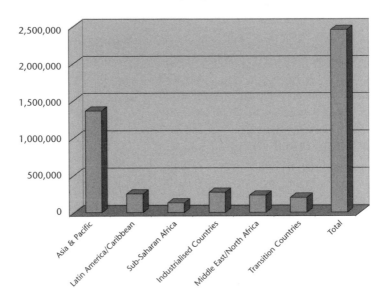

Forced labour by Region – Trafficking Profits ($ Million)

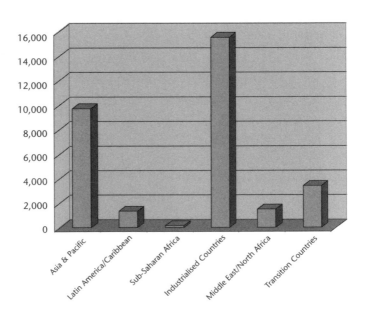

Forced Economic Exploitation by Sex – %

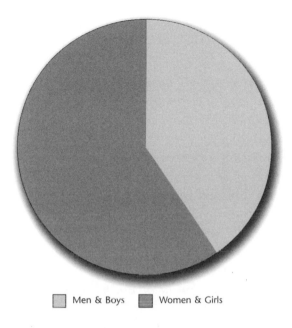

☐ Men & Boys   ▨ Women & Girls

Forced Commercial Sexual Exploitation by Sex

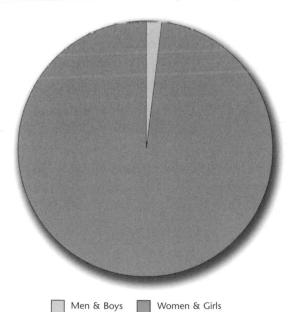

☐ Men & Boys   ▨ Women & Girls

Burma is a source country for women and men trafficked for the purposes of forced labor and sexual exploitation. Burmese men, women, and children (primarily from the country's ethnic minority populations) are trafficked to Thailand, China, Bangladesh, Taiwan, India, Malaysia, Korea, Macau, and Japan for forced labor including commercial labor involuntary domestic servitude, and sexual exploitation. To a lesser extent, Burma is a destination for women from the People's Republic of China (PRC) who are trafficked for commercial sexual exploitation. Internal trafficking of women and girls for sexual exploitation occurs from villages to urban centers and other areas, such as truck stops, fishing villages, border towns, and mining and military camps. The junta's policy of using forced labor is a driving factor behind Burma's large trafficking problem.

The Government of Burma does not fully comply with the minimum standards for the elimination of trafficking and is not making significant efforts to do so. While Burma has made improved efforts to combat trafficking for sexual exploitation, significant state-sanctioned use (especially by the military) of forced labor continued. The Burmese armed forces continued to force ethnic minorities to serve as porters during military operations in ethnic areas. There also are continuing reports that some children were forced to join the Burmese Army. Although eight local officials were convicted in January 2005 on charges of forced labor, the Burmese Government supported or tolerated the use of forced labor for large infrastructure projects. The government sentenced three individuals to death for communicating with the ILO on the subject of forced labor. Because of the Burmese Government's failure to end forced labor, the ILO postponed implementation of a plan of action to address such practices. During the reporting period, the government took some steps to combat trafficking for sexual

*exploitation, including drafting anti-trafficking legislation
and improving cooperation with UN agencies, neighbor-
ing countries, and NGOs.*[5]

Sex Slaves and Human Trafficking

Another form of forced labour occurs where vulnerable people, trapped in poverty in places where unemployment is so
endemic that they can see no way out of the poverty trap, are
lured by offers of work and a better life to leave home and
accept promises that prove to be cruelly false. Once away from
home they may be ruthlessly exploited; if taken abroad they
may have their passports taken; they are often subjected to
imprisonment and physical maltreatment.

Examples of this form of enslavement include those who
are lured into prostitution. They are often very young and
become "sex slaves". Sometimes, their families may sell them
to traffickers who may reassure the parents that they will provide a better quality of life for their child than would ever be
available in their own home area. In other situations, husbands, fathers or brothers may force a girl into prostitution to
earn money for them to pay off their loans to local money-
lenders. Such sex slavery is found in many parts of the world,
including South Asia, India and Europe.

A growing cause of concern is the trafficking in young
women from countries in the former Soviet Union to other
European countries, including the UK. In the USA, the CIA
estimates that as many as 50–60,000 girls and women may be
brought in as slaves for sexual exploitation every year.[6, 7]

According to Naim:

> *...the governments, international organisations, and
> activist groups that track these flows agree on one thing: the
> number of people crossing borders illegally today, often in
> coerced conditions, has no precedent in human history...*

> ...*according to the United Nations, when trafficking and human smuggling are combined an overall picture emerges of a "people trade" that affects at least 4 million people every year, for a value of $7 to $10 billion.*

Moreover:

> *The terms human smuggling and trafficking designate, in principle, two different activities. In human smuggling, the migrant pays the smuggler for passage. In the case of trafficking, the trafficker deceives or coerces the migrant and sells his or her labour.*[8]

In addition:

> *The profits from human trafficking fuel other criminal activities. According to the US Federal Bureau of Investigation, human trafficking generates an estimated $9.5 billion in annual revenue. It is closely connected with money laundering, drug trafficking, document forgery, and human smuggling.*[9]

And:

> *...of the estimated 600,000 to 800,000 people trafficked across international borders annually, 80% of victims are female, and up to 50% are children. Hundreds of thousands of these women and children are used in prostitution each year.*[10]

We now turn to some of the causes and justifications of different types of modern slavery.

CHAPTER SIX

Causes and Justifications
of Modern Slavery

It will be clear that many forms of contemporary slavery are associated with different but often interrelated causes: economic, political and ideological.

Economic

Debt bondage is clearly predominantly economic, being primarily found in situations where individuals or families are being forced to work to try to escape from financial obligations, which may be passed on from one generation to another. Sex slavery is often associated with poverty, in situations where families are so desperate that they will sell their girls into exploitative situations, or allow themselves to be conned into believing that their women will have a better quality of life if they entrust them to the traffickers. In such situations, relief of poverty may remove a primary factor in the persistence of modern slavery, and campaigns such as "Make Poverty History" could help to reduce the vulnerability of impoverished people to enslavement.

Political

However, other forms of slavery may be motivated by political agendas, such as the attempted ethnic cleansing being perpetrated by the SPDC against ethnic national groups. The forced labour inflicted on the Karen, Karenni, Shan, Chin and other peoples is part of a deadly campaign to destroy their communities. Countless villagers have had to flee from their homes and homeland, as they could no longer survive these conditions of exploitation and brutal treatment. The combination of forced labour, military offensives and other gross violations of human rights have resulted in the clearance of vast tracts of Karen, Karenni and Shan States, while many of the peoples of Chin and Kachin States have also fled from conditions that have become intolerable. In Chapter Three we gave details of their experiences.

Ideological

Some forms of slavery may be ideologically justified. The most common contemporary form of ideologically legitimated slavery is found in areas where militant Islam is waging jihad (Islamic holy war), as in Sudan. Over the centuries, military jihad has been associated with slavery and the teachings of traditional Islam have been used to encourage the enslavement of non-Muslims. Many of the case studies described in Chapter One illustrate this form of modern slavery – of Africans by Arabs and of non-Muslims by Muslims.

This form of ideological slavery is so little studied and understood – and so important for the future course of slavery in the twenty-first century – that we now turn to this topic in more detail.

Islam and Slavery – The Historical and Ideological Background

Slavery has been associated with many Islamic societies for more than a thousand years and continues to be so into the twenty-first century.[1] Yet, as we saw in Chapter Four, relatively little has been written about it. Bernard Lewis suggests that:

> *perhaps the main reason for the lack of scholarly research on Islamic slavery is the extreme sensitivity of the subject. This makes it difficult, and sometimes professionally hazardous, for a young scholar to turn his attention in this direction. In time, we may hope, it will be possible for Muslim scholars to examine and discuss Islamic slavery as freely and as openly as European and American scholars have, with the cooperation of scholars from other countries, been willing to discuss this unhappy chapter in their own past. But that time is not yet; meanwhile, Islamic slavery remains both an obscure and a highly sensitive topic, the mere mention of which is often seen as a sign of hostile intentions.[2]*

In Chapter One we have documented in detail the contemporary tragedy of slavery in Sudan, because the scale and intensity of human suffering merits urgent attention and intervention.

In this chapter we outline the ideological background to slavery in the Islamic world and its historical development from the seventh century – the time of Mohammed – to the present. In doing so we will quote extensively from the relatively few authoritative works on the subject.

Discussing the wider implications allows us to consider the moral, religious and political implications for the people of Sudan and for the international community of the Islamist policies adopted by the National Islamic Front (NIF) regime for the Islamisation of Africa using violent jihad and slavery.

The Koran, Islamic Law (Shariah) and Slavery

As we saw in Chapter Four, the Koran recognises the basic inequality between master and slave and the rights of the former over the latter (Sura 16:71; Sura 30:28). It also recognises concubinage (Sura 4:3; Sura 23:6; Suras 33:50–52; Sura 70:30).

Moreover, there are strong links between the traditional Islamic doctrines of military jihad and slavery. According to the Koran:

> When you meet the unbelievers [in a jihad], smite their necks, then, when you have made wide slaughter among them, tie fast the bonds [of slavery].[3]

Any unbelievers captured in militaristic jihad may legitimately be enslaved, and in fact frequently were.

There are three main legitimate sources of slaves in Islam – capture in jihad, birth to slave parents or purchase. However, capture in jihad was by far the most important.

Hence, since jihad is permitted only against non-Muslims, only non-Muslims – predominantly Jews and Christians – are potential slaves.

In practice, men were killed in jihad while women and children were enslaved.[4] As Islamic authority has it – echoing all the preceding legal rulings:

> Make jihad against the infidels, kill their men, make captive their women and children, seize their wealth.[5]

Moreover, both Mohammed and his contemporary Companions are known to have owned many slaves:

> Abde al-Rahman ibn 'Awf, one of the ten closest Companions of the Prophet of Islam, is said to have freed, on his death in 652, no less than thirty thousand slaves.[6]

The result was that slavery (and the enslavement of blacks in particular) became deeply entrenched in Muslim culture and practice:

> ...right from the conquest of Egypt by Arab armies between 639 and 642 CE, the "land of the Blacks", bilad al-Sudan, became a reservoir of slaves for the Muslim world.[7]

Recruitment of Slaves

The main sources were by capture – either by jihad, raids or kidnapping – by tribute or by purchase.[8]

During the early expansion of Islam capture was the primary source but with the spread of Islam, and the increasing number of Jews and Christians who accepted second class or dhimmi status under Islamic rule, the opportunities for further capture were diminished.[9]

An early example of slaves as part of the tribute required from vassal states is a treaty in 652 AD with the black king of Nubia, which included an annual levy of slaves. Similar agreements were imposed by the early Arab conquerors on neighbouring princes in Iran and Central Asia.

Purchase was another method of recruitment, which gradually became the most important source:

> ...slaves were purchased on the frontiers of the Islamic world and then imported to the major cities, where there were slave markets from which they were widely distributed.[10]

Where did the slaves come from?

Slaves in the Islamic lands came from far and wide – initially from the conquered lands in the Middle East, Egypt, Iran, North Africa, Spain, Central Asia and India. Later, most slaves were imported:

> ...from the lands immediately north and south of the Islamic world – whites from Europe and the Eurasian steppes, blacks from Africa south of the Sahara...[11]

From the seventh century onwards many black African slaves were brought by Muslim Arabs to Islamic centres such as Basra, Baghdad, Damascus, Persia, the Arabian peninsula and Egypt.[12]

By which routes did the slaves come?

Initially, black slaves came from West Africa across the Sahara desert to North Africa, and from East Africa down the Nile to Egypt or across the seas to Arabia and Persia.[13]

Later, during early Ottoman times, a major source was white slaves from the Caucasus and the Crimea and even later from the Balkans. However, when these sources were inhibited by the rise of Russia as a military power in the eighteenth century, the Ottomans developed a trade in black slaves from Africa.

The extensive and widespread use of slaves in the Islamic world – in contrast to the largely local focus of slavery in the Ancient world – led to the development of extended networks of slave raiders to provide the slaves and slave traders to bring them to where they were needed.

Nearly every major Islamic city had its slave market, and many continued into the nineteenth century and even, in some cases, into the twentieth century.[14]

Slave Soldiers

In Chapter Four we briefly discussed the use of slaves as soldiers within Islam. Some were captured, as before, but most were bought on the frontiers of Islam, such as the Turks from Central Asia who later made up most of the Muslim armies – officers and commanders as well as ordinary soldiers.

Some became slave kings, like the Mamelukes in Egypt. Over time the Ottomans became substantially dependent on the Janissaries – as the corps of slave soldiers were called – and most Ottoman sultans had slave mothers.[15]

Ibn Khaldun

Ibn Khaldun (1332–1406) was, in some estimations, the greatest of all Arab Muslim historians; his extensive writings had some of the elements of sociology – a discipline which did not start to appear in Europe for another four centuries. His masterpiece *The Muqaddimah: An Introduction to History* dates from 1381.

For Ibn Khaldun, the Turkish slaves were evidence of God's concern for Muslims. He writes of the decadence of the Muslim state under the Abbasids and of how the Turkish slaves rescued Islam by their vigour and dynamism. He thus glories in the institution of slavery which "...hides in itself a divine blessing". Of the imported Turkish slaves he writes:

> ...*one intake comes after another and generation follows generation, and Islam rejoices in the benefit which it gains through them, and the branches of the kingdom flourish with the freshness of youth.*[16]

Ibn Khaldun also wrote that blacks are "...only humans who are closer to dumb animals than to rational beings". They are excitable and emotional due to the "animal spirit" within them and hence are more "wild animals" than "human beings". Thus the Negro nations are generally submissive to slavery because they have little that is essentially human. Moreover:

> *Ibn Khaldun... accepts another contemporary notion that the hot climatic conditions of tropical Africa are what accounts for the colour and debased characteristics of black people.*[17]

Islamic Slavery in Africa after 1400

Before 1450 the Islamic world was virtually the only major external influence on African society.[18] One significant effect of this was the importance of slavery and the slave trade in Africa from 1400 onwards, particularly in the southern Sahara, the Red Sea and East Africa. Islam was a major force in this process both because of its traditional influence in the region and because the chief demand for slaves came from the Muslim states of North Africa and the Middle East.[19]

Lovejoy estimates that the scale of the Medieval Islamic

slave trade in Africa was about "...5,000 to 10,000 slaves per year for centuries before 1600". He cites estimates of nearly 5 million "...for the Saharan trade between 650 and 1600" and nearly 2.5 million "...for the Red Sea and Indian Ocean trade between 800 and 1600" – figures which are a rough approximation and may range in total from 3.5 to 10 million.

The trade was driven by demand from the Islamic world and helped to spread Islamic law, including its treatment of slavery, in sub-Saharan Africa.[20]

White Slavery in North Africa 1500–1800

The first comprehensive study[21] of white slaves taken by corsairs from North Africa and the resulting white slave population of North Africa shows that such slaving exceeded the transatlantic slave trade during the sixteenth and early seventeenth centuries.[22]

Davis has conducted a detailed study of the taking of white slaves from the Mediterranean and the Atlantic coast of Europe by corsairs (or pirates) from North Africa between the sixteenth and the eighteenth century and has also compiled a list of all the available slave counts for this period. Davis also describes how, in the early seventeenth century, some Barbary corsairs sailed up the English Channel and into the Thames estuary. According to Hansard, "...the fishermen are afraid to put to sea, and we are forced to keep continual watches on all our coasts". Even in the second half of the seventeenth century Algerian corsairs are estimated to have enslaved several hundred new British slaves every year.[23]

Davis concludes that between 1530 and 1780 about a million white European Christians were enslaved by Muslims from the Barbary coast, and that:

> ...for most of the first two centuries of the modern era, nearly as many Europeans were taken forcibly to Barbary

and worked or sold as slaves as were West Africans hauled off to labor on plantations in the Americas.[24]

Eighteenth- and Nineteenth-century Africa

Azumah describes how, in the eighteenth and nineteenth centuries:

> ...*the trans-Saharan slave trade increased in volume... Ottoman rulers in league with Muslim Bornu transported large numbers of slaves across the Sahara into the then Ottoman Empire. Many eyewitness accounts talk of substantial loss of lives during the raids and journeys into servitude.*[25]

At the same time there were violent changes within Africa:

> ...*from Senegambia in the west to the Red Sea in the east, the series of holy wars (jihads) that began in 1804 transformed most of this region, and slavery played a vital role in the transformation. The increased importance of slavery is evident in the export figures for slaves – 1,650,000 slaves sold north across the Sahara Desert and the Red Sea but the jihads resulted in the enslavement of millions of other people who were settled within the new states.*

One result was a substantial increase in the use of slaves in productive labour.[26]

Overall, the scale of the intra-African slave trade may have been substantially greater in total than that of the Atlantic slave trade, which peaked in the eighteenth century and was gradually abolished from the early nineteenth century onwards.

> *Apart from the high loss of lives during the raids and journeys, conservative estimates suggest that between eleven and fourteen million Africans were transported into Muslim lands.*[27]

The essential tolerance and hospitality of the indigenous African peoples allowed the early Muslim émigrés to settle in their midst and to establish their Islamic way of life. However, their benign pluralism hindered their conversion to an absolutist religion and prompted frustrated Muslim leaders to resort to "jihad" in its most violent and militaristic forms, and hence to slavery.

Azumah documents in chilling detail the horrific and massive enslavement of Africans by Arabs and analyses the historic role of military jihad. For some Muslim groups, military jihad was the only way to replace the indigenous African environment. For the African jihadists their policy was "...profoundly rooted in the Islamic tradition". The purpose of jihad was "...exalting and promoting Islam for the benefit of humanity in general".

> In seeking to exalt and promote Islam, the jihadists had to subdue the traditional African environment, its people and worldview by dint of arms. Traditional Africans and their socio-religious and political symbols and structures therefore became the principal targets of the jihadists.[28]

There is much evidence from contemporary, mainly European, observers of how "...African slaves were caught, transported, and sold in the markets of the Middle East and North Africa".

This expansion of the African trade was probably due to the growing Russian domination of Eastern Europe and their annexation of the Crimea in 1783, which caused the centuries-old trade of the Tatars to come to an end:

> ...after the Russian annexation of the Caucasian lands circa 1801–28, the last remaining source of white slaves for the Islamic world was reduced and finally stopped. Deprived of their Georgians and Circassians, the Muslim states turned elsewhere, and a large-scale revival of slaving in black Africa took place...

...using the classical routes developed in earlier centuries.[29]

Slavery in the Hijaz and Sudan

The Hijaz – the part of modern Saudi Arabia containing Mecca and Jeddah – was not subject to Ottoman decrees restricting slavery, which gave a new lease of life to the slave market of Mecca. Slaves were imported from East Africa and sent to the north and even to Egypt. The British vice-consul in Damascus reported on March 17, 1877 that:

> Having brought to the notice of the new Governor General, Zia Pasha, the practice of importing African slaves from the markets of Mecca, with the [Pilgrim] Caravan, for sale in Syria, His Excellency informed me that he had already given very strict orders to prevent such abuses.
>
> His Excellency's orders have not, however, met with the success which he stated to me he expected, as slaves were brought as usual.

Slaves were also exported from the Sudan, down the Nile to Egypt and across the Red Sea to Arabia, as they had been from time immemorial. This route was first suppressed by Britain and Egypt, partially restored after the Mahdist revolt in Sudan in the 1890s, and suppressed again by Britain and Egypt in 1896–98.[30]

Treatment of Slaves and the Abolition of the Slave Trade and Slavery

Most black slaves ended up in domestic households where the evidence is that they were well treated. But "...they suffered terribly at the hands and under the lash of slavers and slave dealers from capture until final sale..."[31]

In the nineteenth century the moves to abolish slavery in Europe began to affect slavery within Islam – not to abolish it but initially to restrict and ultimately to abolish the slave trade, which often imposed the worst hardships. Thus

European opponents of slavery focused on the elimination of the slave trade, particularly in Africa.

To abolish slavery itself within Islam would not have been feasible, because for Muslims:

> ...to forbid what God permits is almost as great an offense as to permit what God forbids – and slavery was authorized and regulated by the holy law.

This is why the strongest resistance to any reform came from traditional religious opinion in cities like Mecca and Medina.[32]

Nevertheless, slavery in many Muslim countries was reduced and eventually eliminated almost always because of pressure from Europe.

> In the British, French, Dutch, and Russian Empires – in that order – general abolition had been imposed by the imperial authorities. Britain also undertook, by diplomatic pressure supported by naval power, to suppress the slave trade from East Africa to the Middle East and exacted decrees to this end from the sultan of Turkey, the shah of Persia, and the khedive of Egypt, as well as from a number of local rulers in Africa and Arabia.[33]

In 1857 the Ottoman Empire banned the trade in black slaves but the trade to the Hijaz was exempted to try to stave off a rebellion in the southern provinces of the Empire. However, enforcing the ban was not easy, particularly in the Red Sea area, where the Hijaz exemption proved troublesome, and in Libya, which, towards the end of the nineteenth century, was the only part of Ottoman North Africa not under European rule.

Arabia remained the other major centre, but gradually the Red Sea slave trade shrank following wars in Sudan and Ethiopia and the assumption of British, French and Italian control of the Horn of Africa.

Nevertheless, despite "...the reconquest of the Sudan and all the efforts by Turkish, Egyptian, British, French and

Italian authorities, the traffic continued into modern times...", albeit clandestinely from the 1890s onwards.

But "...the capture, sale and transportation of blacks from Africa to Arabia and Iran continued, however, albeit on a much reduced scale, at least until the mid-twentieth century."[34]

Later – between the two World Wars – most Muslim states in the Middle East abolished chattel slavery, followed in 1960 by Yemen and Saudi Arabia and in 1980 by Mauritania. However:

> *There are persistent reports that despite these legal measures, slavery, sometimes voluntary, continues in several countries.*[35]

Moreover, abolition of the slave trade and of chattel slavery is one thing, but it does not solve the problem of what to do with existing slaves, for whom there was rarely a definite decision for their liberation.

Frequently in Africa, slaves freed themselves by escaping even before colonial conquest. Then:

> *...at the moment of conquest, much larger numbers of slaves took the opportunity to escape, and were sometimes given encouragement to do so by the invaders.*

For example:

> *...when the British took Lagos in 1851 to end slave exports, hundreds of fugitive slaves began to take refuge under the British flag each year... (while) ...after the British defeat of Asante in 1874, thousands of slaves escaped their masters and came to seek their futures in British-ruled towns and at mission stations.*[36]

The Sokoto Caliphate – comprising modern Burkina Faso in the west, through Niger and northern Nigeria to Cameroun in the east – had during the nineteenth century acquired (by capture in war, slave raids and tribute) a huge slave population:

> *...certainly in excess of 1 million and perhaps more than 2.5 million people.*

Hence slavery was still flourishing when the colonial conquest began, people were still being enslaved, and a considerable slave trade still existed.

This meant that:

> *...when the British abolished the legal status of slavery for those parts of the Caliphate that were to become Northern Nigeria, they were dealing with a slave population the scale of which was huge even by the standards of the slave economies of the Americas.*[37]

Moreover:

> *...despite claims that slavery had died or was almost dead, the institution persisted in modified form into the 1930s.*[38]

Where slavery has been abolished or diminished in Islamic societies, this has almost always been at the instigation of or under pressure from colonial European powers:

> *The anti-slavery measures of European colonial powers were generally viewed by Muslims not only as a threat to their very livelihood but also an affront to their religion... Muslims therefore resisted all abolition efforts and chattel slavery persists in Muslim countries today.*[39]

A fascinating debate in the House of Lords in 1960 provided first-hand evidence of slavery and the slave trade in Africa and Arabia in the mid-twentieth century.[40] Lord Shackleton in introducing the debate said:

> *...the chief centre of slavery in the world is still the Arabian Peninsula, and in particular Saudi-Arabia, where it is estimated – and I must stress that it is only an estimate, and may be a very rough one – that there may be as many as half a million slaves to-day.*

> *...it is still practised in not merely Arabia but also the Yemen, Muscat, Oman and the small sheikdoms and sultanates in the Aden Protectorate. There is an abundance of evidence from unofficial sources, from travellers and residents in Saudi-Arabia and those countries, that slavery exists there, and may, indeed, be increasing.*[41]

More recently, in a report presented by the Secretary-General to the United Nations General Assembly in October 1995, the abduction and traffic of young boys and girls from southern Sudan to the northern part of the country for sale as servants and concubines is highlighted in several paragraphs.[42]

And recent studies show that in northern Nigeria:

> *...people can still be found who are considered slaves... The death of slavery, pronounced by so many observers, has been a protracted one and is still not over.*[43]

For many Arabs, slavery is still an uncomfortable subject. As Gordon puts it:

> *...to speak out against it would be to impugn a tenet of Koranic law; to condone slavery would give offence to Africans whose ancestors and not-too-distant relatives in recent times fell victim to Arab slave traders and their agents. As a result, they instinctively keep silent on the subject, which to this day is a source of pain and humiliation for many Africans.*[44]

And there are those in the Islamic world who still, in the twenty-first century, continue to advocate and defend slavery. According to Daniel Pipes, Sheikh Saleh Al-Fawzan, the author of a religious textbook widely used in Saudi schools both in Saudi Arabia and abroad, announced in a recent lecture:

> *"Slavery is a part of Islam... Slavery is part of jihad, and jihad will remain as long there is Islam." He argued against the idea that slavery had ever been abolished, insulting those who espouse this view as "ignorant, not*

scholars. They are merely writers. Whoever says such things is an infidel." [45]

CHAPTER SEVEN

Breaking the Bonds

If slavery is to be abolished in the twenty-first century, we need first to break the bonds of ignorance, silence, interest, ideology, complacency and complicity.

Bonds of ignorance

Far too many people are unaware of the examples of slavery – old and new – that we have discussed in this book. Nor are they aware that the number of slaves is increasing not decreasing in the twenty-first century. Nor do they know that the types of slavery are also increasing. This ignorance needs to be remedied, so that the public are better informed and can bring pressure to bear on the media to expose it and on governments to stop it.

Bonds of silence

Many forms of modern slavery are not mentioned in some quarters because to do so might upset governments or major international organisations. The refusal of the NIF regime in Sudan and the SPDC regime in Burma to allow international aid organisations to go to large areas of countries where slavery is practised is typical of regimes that are perpetrating major abuses of human rights, while being allowed to censor information about these abuses or restrict access to those who suffer from them.

Bonds of interest

Breaking the bonds of interest must involve challenging those who fail to acknowledge or address the well-documented examples described in this book because they think that other matters are more important or because over the years they have failed to act where action was needed. One major example is the United Nations, which, despite issuing clarion calls about the fiftieth anniversary of the Universal Declaration of Human Rights (UDHR) in 1998, has failed to reform the Human Rights Commission whose recent membership has included Sudan, Cuba, Libya, Saudi Arabia and Syria – five of the ten countries rated the "worst of the worst" in Freedom House's annual survey of political rights and civil liberties. In 2005 Sudan's membership was further renewed until 2007.

Other forms of "interest" include commercial interests where economic investment supports, directly or indirectly, regimes that perpetrate slavery.

Bonds of ideology

Silence about the main ideological justification of modern slavery is largely connected with the unwillingness of many in the West to engage in a realistic public debate about the ideology promoted by modern Islamism, which still legitimates slavery. Also, there is often reluctance, in political or religious dialogue with the representatives of the Islamic world, to discuss a realistic account of Islamic ideological justifications of slavery over the last 1,400 years.

Bonds of complacency

It is too easy for us in the West to withdraw into our comfort zones and suggest that it is someone else who should be dealing with the problems of injustice and oppression. We need to remember with John Donne:

> No man is an Island, intire of it selfe;
> every man is a piece of the Continent, a part of the
>   maine;
> if a Clod bee washed away by the Sea, Europe is the
>   lesse,...
> any mans death diminishes me, because I am involved
>   in Mankinde;
> And therefore never send to know for whom the bell tolls;
>   It tolls for thee.[1]

Similarly, freedom is indivisible, and every person denied freedom diminishes our freedom and challenges us to use our freedom to try to achieve theirs.

Bonds of complicity

Once again it is often large organisations – international companies and governments – that turn a blind eye to the injustices we describe. Examples include oil companies in Sudan, or the inadequate response of many governments, including the British government; or the ASEAN nations who have failed to act effectively against Burma.

Bonds of the enslaved

Unless we can break such bonds of ignorance, silence, interest, ideology, complacency and complicity, we will never break the bonds of the enslaved.

As we commemorate William Wilberforce's courage, faith and dedication, which underpinned his parliamentary achievements, we must be challenged to complete the work he began.

What then must we do?

But the question remains as to what specific actions we must or could take to achieve this.

Here we could learn directly from Wilberforce. His key ingredients were publicity and the use of Parliament, backed by national and international diplomacy and the power of the British navy and the British Empire in the nineteenth century.

The analogies today are – once again – publicity, the use of Parliament and similar bodies both national and international, and the use of diplomacy to achieve international agreements, backed where necessary by the threat of sanctions or, as a last resort, force.

Publicity and Parliaments

We have resources of communication undreamt of by Wilberforce two hundred years ago. Let us use them to the full for good, just as the modern slave traders use them for evil.

There are numerous organisations campaigning against modern slavery in its many manifestations and they all provide substantial information on the Internet. We have already mentioned some of them in Chapter Five. They include:

- American Anti-Slavery Group at http://www.iabolish. com ;
- Abolish Slavery – Soon at http://uk.geocities.com/ abolishslaverysoon/ ;
- Anti-Slavery International at http://www.antislavery. org/ ;
- Set All Free at http://www.setallfree.net/ ;
- Coalition to abolish Slavery and Trafficking at http:// www.castla.org/

Use these organisations and others you may find for information and guides to action.

But as well as private organisations let us try to use the power of governments, just as Wilberforce did. One way to do this is to lobby your MP – by both letter and e-mail (always send a copy – of letter or e-mail – to the local press) and by attending the weekly "surgery" they all hold. Try to get them to raise the matter in Parliament and thus bring pressure to bear on the government for effective action. Better still, get MPs to visit some of the countries involved, publish reports when they get back and then ask questions or initiate informative debates in Parliament. And don't forget your Euro MP and the European Parliament – try the same tactics there as well. British foreign policy is now part of EU foreign policy – so it is important to remember the European dimension of advocacy.

National and International Diplomacy

We now have international agreements and organisations again undreamt of in Wilberforce's time. We have already mentioned the Slavery Convention of 1927 and the Universal Declaration of Human Rights (UDHR) adopted by the United Nations in 1948. And there are international and national organisations, such as the International Labour Organisation (ILO) and the US State Department, which is required by United States Congress to publish its *Trafficking in Persons*

Report each year. Let us read their reports, use them and disseminate them as widely as possible.

The most fundamental international agreement is the Universal Declaration of Human Rights of 1948, which was agreed to by all UN members with the solitary exception of Saudi Arabia. Yet many of its provisions, including Article 4 on slavery, are disregarded by many member countries, as the reports mentioned in the previous paragraph make clear.

It is time to call such nations to account and to bring meaningful pressure to bear on them to change their ways either within the UN or without.

Linkage – An idea whose time has come

Perhaps the time has also come to reinvigorate the principle of linkage in national and international policies, in which desirable incentives such as aid are linked to progress on human rights. The best-known recent examples of such linkage are, nationally, the Jackson–Vanik Amendment in the US Congress, which linked US trade benefits to the emigration and human-rights policies of Communist or formerly Communist countries, and, internationally, the Helsinki agreements of 1975 between the former Soviet Union and its satellites and the countries of NATO. The Helsinki agreements were primarily about disarmament, involving nuclear weapons and ballistic missiles, and economic issues. But they contained – in what was called Basket 3 – provisions concerning individual freedoms which in later years were skilfully and courageously used by human-rights activists in Eastern Europe, most notably by Charter 77 in former Czechoslovakia, to draw continual attention to violations of these legally binding agreements. This placed the Communist authorities on the defensive and they were forced to begin to speak the language of law and due process rather than that of force and arbitrary power. It is to this development that the numerous still-existing Helsinki human-rights monitoring groups owe their origins and their names.

It should be possible to use the principle of linkage to make progress in identifying, reducing and eventually eliminating the scourge of slavery from the world.

The campaign for the end of apartheid

Finally, we have a dream. Remember the lengthy and difficult campaign to eliminate apartheid from South Africa. In this campaign, organisations around the world – political, religious, secular, feminist, human rights, you name it – united to bring moral pressure backed by international demonstrations and sanctions in order to hasten the end of apartheid.

Our dream is a similar movement – with similar widespread backing from both grassroots and governments – to end the appalling evil and moral shame of modern twenty-first-century slavery.

There could be no better way to celebrate Wilberforce's political victory than to work tirelessly towards completing the mission to which he dedicated his life: the abolition of slavery from the face of the earth.

Notes

Introduction

1. William Wilberforce, Wikipedia, www.wikipedia.com.

2. D. Vaughan, Statesman and Saint, *The Principled Politics of William Wilberforce*, Highland Press, 2002.

3. P. Hammond, *The Scourge of Slavery*, Christian Action, 2004.

4. P. Hammond, *The Scourge of Slavery*, Christian Action, 2004.

5. D. Vaughan, Statesman and Saint, *The Principled Politics of William Wilberforce*, Highland Press, 2002.

Chapter One: Let the Slaves of Sudan Speak

1. These visits were undertaken with a number of different organisations – especially with CSI (Christian Solidarity International) in the earlier years and then with CSW (Christian Solidarity Worldwide).

2. Media references: Tim Sandler "Africa's Invisible Slaves. An Outrage the World Ignores", *The Boston Phoenix*, June 30–July 6, 1995; Gilbert Lewthwaite and Gregory Kane, "Witness to Slavery", *The Baltimore Sun*, June 16–18, 1996; Ricardo Orizio, "Ho assistito alla tratta dei neri, 180 mila lire per uno schiavo", *Corriere della Sera*, February 17, 1998; Damien Lewis, *It's Not Famine, It's Genocide*, Channel 4, 1998; *Slavery in Sudan*, NBC Dateline, 1998;

BBC *Everyman* Programme: "The Dangerous Adventures of Baroness Cox", January 29, 2001.

3. Hasan al-Turabi is the main ideological inspiration of the Islamist NIF regime; Caroline Cox had a lengthy meeting with him in Khartoum in 1993.

4. We were told that the price could vary: the average was five cows per person, but in some cases it could rise to a maximum of fifteen.

5. The SPLA was the largest opposition army, led by Dr John Garang, who subsequently became Vice-President of Sudan after the signing of the Comprehensive Peace Agreement until he was killed in a helicopter crash in 2005; the civilian parallel organisation, the SPLM (Sudadese People's Liberation Movement) would assume responsibility for civil administration and the development of civil society in areas controlled by the SPLA.

Chapter Three: Let the Sex Slaves, Forced Porters and Child Soldiers of Burma Speak

1. *Catwalk to the Barracks: Conscription of Women for Sexual Slavery and Other Practices of Sexual Violence by Troops of the Burmese Military Regime in Mon Areas*, by Woman and Child Rights Project (Southern Burma) in collaboration with Human Rights Foundation of Monland (Burma), July 2005.

2. *License to Rape: The Burmese Military Regime's Use of Sexual Violence in the Ongoing War in Shan State*, by The Shan Human Rights Foundation (SHRF) and The Shan Women's Action Network (SWAN), May 2002.

3. *Shattering Silences: Karen Women speak out about the Burmese Military Regime's use of Rape as a Strategy of War in Karen State*, by The Karen Women's Organization (KWO) with the collaboration of The Committee for Internally Displaced Karen People (CIDKP), The Karen Information Center (KIC), The Karen Human Rights Group (KHRG) and The Mergui-Tavoy District Information Department, April 2004.

4. *Driven Away: Trafficking of Kachin Women on the China–Burma Border* by the Kachin Women's Association of Thailand (KWAT), June 2005.

5. Ibid., p. 6.

6. Ibid., p. 49.

7. Ibid., pp. 51–53.

8. See Chapter Five below.

9. *My Gun was as Tall as Me: Child Soldiers in Burma*, Human Rights Watch, October 2002.

10. All names of children, soldiers and former soldiers have been changed.

11. See Chapter Five below.

12. For example, *No Status, Migration, Trafficking and Exploitation of Women in Thailand: Health and HIV/AIDS Risks for Burmese and Hill Tribe Women and Girls*, Physicians for Human Rights, June 2004.

Part Two: Introduction. What is Slavery?

1. Preamble to *Slavery Convention*, 1926.

2. Article 1, *Slavery Convention*.

3. High Commissioner for Human Rights Opening Statement to WGCFS, Geneva, May 1998; related documents can be located at the United Nations Human Rights Documentation Research Guide on the Internet.

Chapter Four: Slavery Through the Ages

1. "slavery." Encyclopaedia Britannica. 2006. Encyclopaedia Britannica Premium Service. Febuary 7, 2006 www.britannica.com/eb/article-9109538>

2. See B. Lewis, *Race and Slavery in the Middle East: An Historical Enquiry*, Oxford University Press, New York, Oxford, 1990; P. Lovejoy, *Transformations in Slavery: A history of slavery in Africa*, Cambridge University Press, 1983; S. Marmon, (ed.), *Slavery in the Islamic Middle East*, Markus Wiener (Princeton), 1999; P. Crone, *Slaves on Horses: The Evolution of the Islamic Polity*, Cambridge University Press, 2003; see further references in Chapter Six.

3. "**slavery.**" Encyclopaedia Britannica. 2006. Encyclopaedia Britannica Premium Service. Febuary 7, 2006 **www.britannica. com/eb/article-9109538**>

4. B. Lewis, *Race and Slavery in the Middle East: An Historical Enquiry*, Oxford University Press, New York, Oxford, 1990, p. 5.

5. Suras 16:71 (Medina) and 30:28 (Medina).

6. Suras 4:3; 23:6; 33:50–52; and 70:30.

7. J. Azumah, *The Legacy of Arab-Islam in Africa – A Quest for Inter-religious Dialogue*, Oxford, 2001, p. 125.

8. Ibid., p. 126.

9. B. Lewis, *Race and Slavery in the Middle East, An Historical Enquiry*, Oxford University Press, 1990, p. iv.

10. D. Waines (trans.), *The Revolt of the Zanj: AD 869–879*; Volume XXXVI of *The History of Al-Tabari*, State University of New York Press, 1992.

11. D. Pipes, *Slave Soldiers and Islam: The Genesis of a Military System*, Yale University Press, 1981, p. 45.

12. Ibid., p. 53.

13. The term "Mameluke" is derived from an Arabic word for slave – usually white slaves: the Arabic word for black slaves is "Abd".

14. J. Azumah, *Islam and Slavery*, Centre for Islamic Studies, London Bible College, 1999, p. 3. See also J. Azumah, *The Legacy of Arab-Islam in Africa*, Oneworld Publications, 2001 for a comprehensive and detailed account of slavery and Islam in Africa, including a discussion of the role of *shari'a* and *Jihad*, from pre-colonial times to the present.

15. See Chapter Six, Causes and Justifications.

16. "slavery." Encyclopaedia Britannica. 2006. Encyclopaedia Britannica Premium Service. Febuary 7, 2006 www.britannica.com/eb/article-9109538>

17. H. Thomas, *The Slave Trade: The History of the Atlantic Slave Trade 1440–1870*, Simon & Schuster, 1997, pp. 805–6; see also the many references cited therein.

18. "slavery." Encyclopaedia Britannica. 2006. Encyclopaedia Britannica Premium Service. Febuary 7, 2006 www.britannica.com/eb/article-9109538>

19. B. Lewis, *Cultures in Conflict: Christians, Muslims, and Jews in the Age of Discovery*, Oxford University Press, 1995. p. 72.

Chapter Five: Contemporary Slavery – Variations on the Theme

1. Section on Sudan in *Trafficking in Persons Report*, June 2005, US State Department.

2. C. Jacobs, *Slavery in the 21st Century*, Year in Review 2000: special report, Encyclopaedia Britannica.

3. *Debt Bondage*, IAbolish Factsheets, 2006.

4. *A Global Alliance Against Forced Labour*, ILO, 2005.

5. Section on Burma in *Trafficking in Persons Report*, June 2005, US State Department.

6. C. Dolan, *A Shattered Innocence: The Millennium Holocaust*, International Humanitarian Campaign Against the Exploitation of Children, April 2001.

7. M. Naim, *Illicit: How Smugglers, Traffickers and Copycats Are Hijacking the Global Economy*, Doubleday, 2005.

8. Ibid., pp. 88–89.

9. *Trafficking in Persons Report*, June 2005, US State Department, pp. 13–14.

10. *Trafficking in Persons Report*, June 2005, US State Department, p. 19.

Chapter Six: Causes and Justifications of Modern Slavery

1. See B. Lewis, *Race and Slavery in the Middle East: An Historical Enquiry*, Oxford University Press, New York, Oxford, 1990; P. Lovejoy, *Transformations in Slavery: A History of Slavery in Africa*, Cambridge University Press, 1983; S. Marmon, (ed.), *Slavery in the Islamic Middle East*, Markus Wiener (Princeton), 1999; P. Crone, *Slaves on Horses: The Evolution of the Islamic Polity*, Cambridge University Press, 1980.

2. B. Lewis, *Race and Slavery in the Middle East, An Historical Enquiry*, Oxford University Press, 1990, p. iv.

3. *Sura 47:4*.

4. J. Azumah, op. cit., pp. 125–6.

5. J. Willis, *Jihad and the Ideology of Enslavement in Islam* in J. Willis (ed.), *Slaves and Slavery in Muslim Africa*, Vol. 1, 1985, p. 22.

6. I. Petrushevsky, *Islam in Iran* (trans. H. Evans), Athlone, 1985, p. 158.

7. J. Azumah, op. cit., p. 141.

8. Ibid., p. 141; see also Y. Hasan, *The Arabs and the Sudan: From the Seventh to the Early Sixteenth Century*, Edinburgh University Press, 1967, p. 134.

9. B. Lewis, op. cit., p. 9.

10. Ibid., p. 10.

11. Ibid., p. 11.

12. Azumah, ibid., pp. 141–2; see also Hunwick, *Black Africans in the Islamic World: An Understudied Dimension of the Black Diaspora* in *Tarikh*, Vol. 5, No. 4, 1978, p. 25.

13. B. Lewis, op. cit., p. 11.

14. Ibid., pp. 12–13; see also the extensive references cited therein.

15. Lewis, op. cit., p. 64.

16. Ibid., p. 65: translation from B. Lewis, *Islam from the Prophet Muhammad to the Capture of Constantinople*, Vol. 1, Oxford University Press, 1974, pp. 97–99.

17. Azumah, op. cit., p. 135; see Ibn Khaldun, *Muqaddimah*, Routledge and Kegan Paul, 1958, pp. 119, 168–9, 174–6 and 301.

18. P. Lovejoy, *Transformations in Slavery: A History of Slavery in Africa (Second Edition)*, Cambridge University Press, 2000, p. 15.

19. Ibid., p. 23.

20. Ibid., p. 24; see also R. Austen, *The trans-Saharan slave trade: A tentative census* in H. Gemery and J. Hogendoorn (eds) *The Uncommon Market: Essays in the Economic History of the Atlantic Slave Trade*, New York, 1979, pp. 66–68.

21. R. Davis, *Christian Slaves, Muslim Masters: White Slavery in the Mediterranean, the Barbary Coast, and Italy, 1500–1800*, Palgrave Macmillan, 2003; see in particular part one, chapters 1 and 2. For a more detailed account of one such slave see, for example, G. Milton, *White Gold: The Extraordinary Story of Thomas Pellow and Islam's One Million White Slaves*, Farrar, Straus and Giroux, 2004.

22. R. Davis, op. cit., p. xxvi.

23. Ibid., pp. 3–4.

24. Ibid., pp. 23, 24.

25. J. Azumah, *Islam and Slavery*, Centre for Islamic Studies, London Bible College, 1999, p. 3.

26. Lovejoy, op. cit., p. 184.

27. M. Gordon, *Slavery in the Arab World*, New Amsterdam Books, 1987, p. ix. The Atlantic slave trade was important from about 1650 to 1850 and peaked just before 1800, whereas the intra-African slave trade started earlier and went on later; its most important years were from 1750 to 1900 with a peak around 1850; see P. Manning, *Slavery and African Life: Occidental, Oriental and African Slave*

Trades, Cambridge University Press, 1990, pp. 9–12; for a comprehensive account of the Atlantic slave trade see H. Thomas, *The Slave Trade: The History of the Atlantic Slave Trade 1440–1870*, Simon & Schuster, 1997, and the many references cited therein.

28. Azumah, pp. 107–8.

29. Lewis, op. cit., pp. 72–3.

30. Ibid., pp. 73–4.

31. Ibid., p. 77.

32. Ibid., p. 78.

33. Ibid, p. 79.

34. Ibid., pp. 81–2.

35. Ibid., p. 79.

36. P. Manning, *Slavery and African Life: Occidental, Oriental, and African Slave Trades*, Cambridge University Press, 1990, pp. 160–1.

37. P. Lovejoy & J. Hogendorn, *Slow Death for Slavery: The Course of Abolition in Northern Nigeria, 1897–1936*, Cambridge University Press, 1993, pp. 1–2.

38. Ibid., pp. 284–5.

39. J. Azumah, *Islam and Slavery*, Centre for Islamic Studies, London Bible College, 1999, p. 5.

40. *Slavery in Africa and Arabia*, House of Lords Hansard, July 14, 1960, Col. 333–356.

41. Ibid., Col. 334.

42. Note presented by the Secretary-General to the 50th Session of the United Nations General Assembly, October 16, 1995.

43. P. Lovejoy and J. Hogendoorn (eds) *Slow Death for Slavery: The Course of Abolition in Northern Nigeria, 1897–1936*, Cambridge University Press, 1993, p. 30.

44. M. Gordon, *Slavery in the Arab World*, New Amsterdam Books, 1987/1992; Introduction to the American Edition; see also R. Segal,

Islam's Black Slaves: The Other Black Diaspora, Farrar, Straus and Giroux, 2001, and P. Manning, *Slavery and African Life: Occidental, Oriental, and African Slave Trades*, Cambridge University Press, 1990.

45. D. Pipes, *Saudi Religious Leader Calls for Slavery's Legalization*, November 7, 2003, www.danielpipes.org/blog/123. Al-Fawzan is a member of the Senior Council of Clerics, Saudi Arabia's highest religious body; a member of the Council of Religious Edicts and Research; Imam of the Prince Mitaeb Mosque in Riyadh; and Professor at Imam Mohamed Bin Saud Islamic University, the main Wahhabi centre of learning.

Chapter Seven: Breaking the Bonds

1. John Donne, Meditation XVII of *Devotions Upon Emergent Occasions*, 1624.

Bibliography

Books

The Scourge of Slavery, Peter Hammond: Cape Town,
Christian Action, 2004.

*Statesman and Saint: The Principled Politics of William
Wilberforce*, David Vaughan: Nashville, Highland Press,
2002.

Race and Slavery in the Middle East: An Historical Enquiry,
Bernard Lewis: Oxford, Oxford University Press, 1990.

Slavery in the Islamic Middle East, Shaun Marmon (ed):
Princeton, Markus Wiener, 1999.

*The Legacy of Arab-Islam in Africa – A Quest for Inter-religious
Dialogue*, John Azumah: Oxford, Oneworld
Publications, 2001.

Slave Soldiers and Islam: The Genesis of a Military System,
Daniel Pipes: New Haven, Yale University Press, 1981.

Islam and Slavery, John Azumah: London, Centre for Islamic
Studies, London School of Theology, 1999.

*The Slave Trade: The History of the Atlantic Slave Trade
1440–1870*, Hugh Thomas: New York, Simon &
Schuster, 1997.

*Cultures in Conflict: Christians, Muslims, and Jews in the Age
of Discovery*, Bernard Lewis: Oxford, Oxford University
Press, 1995.

A Shattered Innocence: The Millennium Holocaust, Christine
  Dolan: Washington, International Humanitarian
  Campaign Against the Exploitation of Children, 2001.
*Illicit: How Smugglers, Traffickers and Copycats Are Hijacking
  the Global Economy*, Moises Naim: New York,
  Doubleday, 2005.
*Transformations in slavery: A history of slavery in Africa
  (Second Edition)*, Paul Lovejoy: Cambridge, Cambridge
  University Press, 2000.
*Christian Slaves, Muslim Masters: White Slavery in the
  Mediterranean, the Barbary Coast, and Italy, 1500–1800*,
  Robert Davis: Basingstoke, Palgrave Macmillan, 2003.
Slavery in the Arab World, Murray Gordon: New York, New
  Amsterdam Books, 1987.
*Slavery and African life: Occidental, Oriental and African Slave
  Trades*, Patrick Manning: Cambridge, Cambridge
  University Press, 1990.
*Slow death for slavery: The course of abolition in Northern
  Nigeria, 1897–1936*, Paul Lovejoy & Jan Hogendorn;
  Cambridge, Cambridge University Press, 1993.
Islam's Black Slaves: The Other Black Diaspora, Ronald Segal:
  New York, Farrar, Straus and Giroux, 2001.
*The 'West', Islam and Islamism: Is ideological Islam
  compatible with liberal democracy*, Caroline Cox and
  John Marks: London, Civitas, Second Edition,
  forthcoming October 2006.

Reports

*Catwalk to the Barracks: Conscription of women for sexual
  slavery and other practices of sexual violence by troops of
  the Burmese military regime in Mon areas*, Woman and
  Child Rights Project (Southern Burma) in
  collaboration with Human Rights Foundation of
  Monland (Burma), July 2005

License to Rape: The Burmese military regime's use of sexual violence in the ongoing war in Shan State, The Shan Human Rights Foundation (SHRF) and The Shan Women's Action Network (SWAN), May 2002

Shattering Silences: Karen Women speak out about the Burmese Military Regime's use of Rape as a Strategy of War in Karen State, The Karen Women's Organization (KWO) with the collaboration of The Committee for Internally Displaced Karen People (CIDKP), The Karen Information Center (KIC), The Karen Human Rights Group (KHRG) and The Mergui-Tavoy District Information Department, April, 2004

Driven Away: Trafficking of Kachin women on the China–Burma border, Kachin Women's Association of Thailand (KWAT), June 2005

My Gun Was A Tall As Me: Child Soldiers in Burma, Human Rights Watch: Chicago, October, 2002.

No Status, Migration, Trafficking and Exploitation of Women in Thailand: Health and HIV/AIDS Risks for Burmese and Hill Tribe Women and Girls, Physicians for Human Rights: Cambridge, MA, June 2004.

Trafficking in Persons Report, US State Department: Washington, June 2005

A Global Alliance Against Forced Labour, International Labour Organisation: Geneva, 2005